AUTOBIOGRAPHICAL
NOTES

AUTOBIOGRAPHICAL NOTES

A CENTENNIAL EDITION

Translated and edited by
Paul Arthur Schilpp
Southern Illinois University at Carbondale

Open ❋ Court

La Salle, Illinois

This book has been reproduced in a print-on-demand format from the 1996 Open Court printing.

To order books from Open Court, call toll-free 1-800-815-2280 or visit our website at www.opencourtbooks.com.

Open Court Publishing Company
is a division of Carus Publishing Company.

First published in *Albert Einstein: Philosopher–Scientist* in *The Library of Living Philosophers*, ed. Paul Arthur Schilpp. First published in this separate edition by Open Court Publishing Company, 1979.

First printing 1979
Second printing 1991/First paperback printing 1991
Second paperback printing 1992
Third paperback printing 1996

Printed and bound in the United States of America.

Albert Einstein: Autobiographical Notes

Library of Congress Catalog Card Number: 78-13925

ISBN: 0-87548-352-6
ISBN: 0-8126-9179-2 (pbk.)

Cover Design: Todd Sanders

Preface

The late Albert Einstein's *Autobiographisches* (Autobiographical Notes) is a unique and precious document. It constitutes the only major attempt Professor Einstein ever made to write anything even approaching an autobiography.[1] For him that meant only relating how his mind developed and how one train of thought and of consideration led to others: in brief, how, when, and why he happened to think as he did and to what conclusions such thinking led him at any specific time. Although it is an eminently personal account, it says almost nothing about his private or family life and almost nothing about the tremendous events that shook the world during his lifetime and encircled his everyday existence. In other words, it is a scientific *Selbst-Darstellung* (self-portrait) by the greatest and most original scientific thinker of the twentieth century.

It was written at the invitation and earnest request of the editor—and I might say it took quite some persuasion—for Volume VII of our *Library of Living Philosophers*, the volume entitled *Albert Einstein: Philosopher-Scientist* (originally published in 1949). Since 1949 it has appeared in English (or even in its original German) only in the various editions of that volume. It is now appearing—again in both languages, side by side—for the first time as a separate volume in commemoration of the hundredth anniversary of Einstein's birth, March 14, 1879.

The English translation, originally made by the editor, has had the benefit of a thorough inspection and (when necessary) revision by Professor Peter Bergmann, noted physicist at Syracuse University, who for five years was Dr. Einstein's scientific assistant at the Institute for Advanced Study in Princeton. Professor Bergmann and the administrators of the Einstein estate, Dr. Otto Nathan and Miss Helen Dukas, have been most courteously helpful, which the editor here gladly and gratefully acknowledges.

And it is, in fact, through the intercession of Dr. Nathan that we are able to reproduce here, as our frontispiece, the beautiful and distinctive photograph by Mr. Philippe Halsman.

Other acknowledgement of appreciation is due the Hegeler Foundation and the administrators of Open Court Publishing Company of La Salle, Illinois, who, in almost record time, succeeded in producing this book in its special holiday format in time for the Einstein centennial, an event that Southern Illinois University at Carbondale is pleased to celebrate during a special "Einstein Week," February 23 through March 3, 1979.

Paul Arthur Schilpp

Carbondale, Illinois

June 1978

---

[1] The minor exception is an eight-page "Autobiographische Skizze," which appeared in Carl Selig's *Helle Zeit–Dunkle Zeit, in Memoriam Albert Einstein* (Europa Verlag, Zürich, 1956, pp. 9–17).

A. Einstein.

AUTOBIOGRAPHICAL
NOTES

Autobiographisches

Hier sitze ich, um mit siebenundsechzig Jahren so etwas wie den eigenen Nekrolog zu schreiben. Dies tue ich nicht nur, weil mich Dr. Schilpp dazu überredet hat; sondern ich glaube selber dass es gut ist, den Mitstrebenden zu zeigen, wie einem das eigene Streben und Suchen im Rückblick erscheint. Nach einiger Überlegung fühlte ich, wie unvollkommen ein solcher Versuch ausfallen muss. Denn wie kurz und beschränkt ein Arbeitsleben ist, wie vorherrschend die Irrwege, so fällt doch die Darstellung des Mitteilungswerten nicht leicht–der jetzige Mensch von siebenundsechzig ist nicht derselbe wie der von fünfzig, dreissig und zwanzig. Jede Erinnerung ist gefärbt durch das jetzige So-Sein, also durch einen trügerischen Blickpunkt. Diese Erwägung könnte wohl abschrecken. Aber man kann doch Manches aus dem Selbst-Erleben schöpfen, was einem andern Bewusstsein nicht zugänglich ist.

Als ziemlich frühreifem jungem Menschen kam mir die Nichtigkeit des Hoffens und Strebens lebhaft zum Bewusstsein, das die meisten Menschen rastlos durchs Leben jagt. Auch sah ich bald die Grausamkeit dieses Treibens, die in jenen Jahren sorgsamer als jetzt durch Hypocrisy und glänzende Worte verdeckt war. Jeder war durch die Existenz seines Magens dazu verurteilt, an diesem Treiben sich zu beteiligen, Der Magen konnte durch solche Teilnahme wohl befriedigt werden, aber nicht der Mensch als denkendes und fühlendes Wesen. Da gab es als ersten Ausweg die Religion, die ja jedem Kinde durch die traditionelle Erziehungs-Maschine eingepflanzt wird. So kam ich–obwohl ein Kind ganz irreligiöser (jüdischer) Eltern– zu einer tiefen Religiosität, die aber im Alter von zwölf Jahren bereits ein jähes Ende fand. Durch Lesen populär-wissenschaftlicher Bücher kam ich bald zu der Überzeugung, dass vieles in den Erzählungen der Bibel nicht wahr sein konnte. Die Folge war eine geradezu

Autobiographical Notes[*]

Here I sit in order to write, at the age of sixty-seven, something like my own obituary. I am doing this not merely because Dr. Schilpp has persuaded me to do it, but because I do, in fact, believe that it is a good thing to show those who are striving alongside of us how our own striving and searching appears in retrospect. After some reflection, I felt how imperfect any such attempt is bound to be. For, however brief and limited one's working life may be, and however predominant may be the way of error, the exposition of that which is worthy of communication does nonetheless not come easy—today's person of sixty-seven is by no means the same as was the one of fifty, of thirty, or of twenty. Every reminiscence is colored by one's present state, hence by a deceptive point of view. This consideration could easily deter one. Nevertheless much can be gathered out of one's own experience that is not open to another consciousness.

When I was a fairly precocious young man I became thoroughly impressed with the futility of the hopes and strivings that chase most men restlessly through life. Moreover, I soon discovered the cruelty of that chase, which in those years was much more carefully covered up by hypocrisy and glittering words than is the case today. By the mere existence of his stomach everyone was condemned to participate in that chase. The stomach might well be satisfied by such participation, but not man insofar as he is a thinking and feeling being. As the first way out there was religion, which is implanted into every child by way of the traditional education-machine. Thus I came—though the child of entirely irreligious (Jewish) parents—to a deep religiousness, which, however, reached an abrupt end at the age of twelve. Through the reading of popular scientific books I soon reached the conviction that much in the stories of the Bible could not be true. The consequence was a positively fanatic [orgy

*Translated from the original German manuscript by Paul Arthur Schilpp and revised with the help of Professor Peter Bergmann of Syracuse University.

fanatische Freigeisterei, verbunden mit dem Eindruck, dass die Jugend vom Staate mit Vorbedacht belogen wird; es war ein niederschmetternder Eindruck. Das Misstrauen gegen jede Art Autorität erwuchs aus diesem Erlebnis, eine skeptische Einstellung gegen die Überzeugungen, welche in der jeweiligen sozialen Umwelt lebendig waren–eine Einstellung, die mich nicht wieder verlassen hat, wenn sie auch später durch bessere Einsicht in die kausalen Zusammenhänge ihre ursprüngliche Schärfe verloren hat.

Es ist mir klar, dass das so verlorene religiöse Paradies der Jugend ein erster Versuch war, mich aus den Fesseln des »Nur-Persönlichen« zu befreien, aus einem Dasein, das durch Wünsche, Hoffnungen und primitive Gefühle beherrscht ist. Da gab es draussen diese grosse Welt, die unabhängig von uns Menschen da ist und vor uns steht wie ein grosses, ewiges Rätsel, wenigstens teilweise zugänglich unserem Schauen und Denken. Ihre Betrachtung winkte als eine Befreiung, und ich merkte bald, dass so Mancher, den ich schätzen und bewundern gelernt hatte, in der hingebenden Beschäftigung mit ihr innere Freiheit und Sicherheit gefunden hatte. Das gedankliche Erfassen dieser ausserpersönlichen Welt im Rahmen der uns gebotenen Möglichkeiten, schwebte mir halb bewusst, halb unbewusst als höchstes Ziel vor. Ähnlich eingestellte Menschen der Gegenwart und Vergangenheit sowie die von ihnen erlangten Einsichten waren die unverlierbaren Freunde. Der Weg zu diesem Paradies war nicht so bequem und lockend wie der Weg zum religiösen Paradies; aber er hat sich als zuverlässig erwiesen, und ich habe es nie bedauert, ihn gewählt zu haben.

Was ich da gesagt habe, ist nur in gewissem Sinne wahr, wie eine aus wenigen Strichen bestehende Zeichnung einem komplizierten, mit verwirrenden Einzelheiten ausgestatteten, Objekt nur in beschränktem Sinne gerecht werden kann. Wenn ein Individuum an gutgefügten Gedanken Freude hat, so mag sich diese Seite seines Wesens auf Kosten anderer Seiten stärker ausprägen und so seine Mentalität in steigendem Masse bestimmen. Es mag dann wohl sein, dass dies Individuum im Rückblick eine einheitliche systematische Entwicklung sieht, während das tatsächliche Erleben in kaleidoskopartiger Einzel-Situation sich abspielt. Die Mannigfaltigkeit der äusseren Situationen und die Enge des momentanen Bewusstsein-

of] freethinking coupled with the impression that youth is intentionally being deceived by the state through lies; it was a crushing impression. Mistrust of every kind of authority grew out of this experience, a skeptical attitude toward the convictions that were alive in any specific social environment–an attitude that has never again left me, even though, later on, it has been tempered by a better insight into the causal connections.

It is quite clear to me that the religious paradise of youth, which was thus lost, was a first attempt to free myself from the chains of the "merely personal," from an existence dominated by wishes, hopes, and primitive feelings. Out yonder there was this huge world, which exists independently of us human beings and which stands before us like a great, eternal riddle, at least partially accessible to our inspection and thinking. The contemplation of this world beckoned as a liberation, and I soon noticed that many a man whom I had learned to esteem and to admire had found inner freedom and security in its pursuit. The mental grasp of this extra-personal world within the frame of our capabilities presented itself to my mind, half consciously, half unconsciously, as a supreme goal. Similarly motivated men of the present and of the past, as well as the insights they had achieved, were the friends who could not be lost. The road to this paradise was not as comfortable and alluring as the road to the religious paradise; but it has shown itself reliable, and I have never regretted having chosen it.

What I have said here is true only in a certain sense, just as a drawing consisting of a few strokes can do justice to a complicated object, full of perplexing details, only in a very limited sense. If an individual enjoys well-ordered thoughts, it is quite possible that this side of his nature may grow more pronounced at the cost of other sides and thus may determine his mentality in increasing degree. In this case it may well be that such an individual sees in retrospect a uniformly systematic development, whereas the actual experience takes place in kaleidoscopic particular situations. The great variety of the external situations and the narrowness of the momentary content of consciousness bring about a sort of atomizing of the life

Inhaltes bringen ja eine Art Atomisierung des Lebens jedes Menschen mit sich. Bei einem Menschen meiner Art liegt der Wendepunkt der Entwicklung darin, dass das Hauptinteresse sich allmählich weitgehend loslösst vom Momentanen und Nur-Persönlichen und sich dem Streben nach gedanklicher Erfassung der Dinge zuwendet. Von diesem Gesichtspunkt aus betrachtet enthalten die obigen schematischen Bemerkungen so viel Wahres, als sich in solcher Kürze sagen lässt.

Was ist eigentlich ›Denken‹? Wenn beim Empfangen von Sinnes-Eindrücken Erinnerungsbilder auftauchen, so ist das noch nicht ›Denken.‹ Wenn solche Bilder Serien bilden, deren jedes Glied ein anderes wachruft, so ist dies auch noch kein ›Denken.‹ Wenn aber ein gewisses Bild in vielen solchen Reihen wiederkehrt, so wird es eben durch seine Wiederkehr zu einem ordnenden Element für solche Reihen, indem es an sich zusammenhangslose Reihen verknüpft. Ein solches Element wird zum Werkzeug, zum Begriff. Ich denke mir, dass der Übergang vom freien Assoziieren oder ›Träumen‹ zum Denken charakterisiert ist durch die mehr oder minder dominierende Rolle, die der ›Begriff‹ dabei spielt. Es ist an sich nicht nötig, dass ein Begriff mit einem sinnlich wahrnehmbaren und reproduzierbaren Zeichen (Wort) verknüpft sei; ist er es aber so wird dadurch Denken mitteilbar.

Mit welchem Recht – so fragt nun der Leser – operiert dieser Mensch so unbekümmert und primitiv mit Ideen auf einem so problematischen Gebiet, ohne den geringsten Versuch zu machen, etwas zu beweisen? Meine Verteidigung: all unser Denken ist von dieser Art eines freien Spiels mit Bergriffen; die Berechtigung dieses Spiels liegt in dem Masse der Übersicht über die Sinnenerlebnisse, die wir mit seiner Hilfe erreichen können. Der Begriff der ›Wahrheit‹ kann auf ein solches Gebilde noch gar nicht angewendet werden; dieser Begriff kann nach meiner Meinung erst dann in Frage kommen, wenn bereits eine weitgehende Einigung (Convention) über die Elemente und Regeln des Spieles vorliegen.

Es ist mir nicht zweifelhaft, dass unser Denken zum grössten Teil ohne Verwendung von Zeichen (Worte) vor sich geht und dazu noch weitgehend unbewusst. Denn wie sollten wir sonst manchmal dazu kommen, uns über ein Erlebnis ganz spontan zu ›wundern‹?

of every human being. In a man of my type, the turning point of the development lies in the fact that gradually the major interest disengages itself to a far-reaching degree from the momentary and the merely personal and turns toward the striving for a conceptual grasp of things. Looked at from this point of view, the above schematic remarks contain as much truth as can be stated with such brevity.

What, precisely, is "thinking"? When, on the reception of sense impressions, memory pictures emerge, this is not yet "thinking." And when such pictures form sequences, each member of which calls forth another, this too is not yet "thinking." When, however, a certain picture turns up in many such sequences, then–precisely by such return–it becomes an organizing element for such sequences, in that it connects sequences in themselves unrelated to each other. Such an element becomes a tool, a concept. I think that the transition from free association or "dreaming" to thinking is characterized by the more or less preeminent role played by the "concept." It is by no means necessary that a concept be tied to a sensorily cognizable and reproducible sign (word); but when this is the case, then thinking becomes thereby capable of being communicated.

With what right–the reader will ask–does this man operate so carelessly and primitively with ideas in such a problematic realm without making even the least effort to prove anything? My defense: all our thinking is of this nature of free play with concepts; the justification for this play lies in the degree of comprehension of our sensations that we are able to achieve with its aid. The concept of "truth" can not yet be applied to such a structure; to my thinking this concept becomes applicable only when a far-reaching agreement (*convention*) concerning the elements and rules of the game is already at hand.

I have no doubt but that our thinking goes on for the most part without use of signs (words) and beyond that to a considerable degree unconsciously. For how, otherwise, should it happen that sometimes we "wonder" quite spontaneously about some experi-

Dies »sich wundern« scheint dann aufzutreten, wenn ein Erlebnis mit einer in uns hinreichend fixierten Begriffswelt in Konflikt kommt. Wenn solcher Konflikt hart und intensiv erlebt wird dann wirkt er in entscheidender Weise zurück auf unsere Gedankenwelt. Die Entwicklung dieser Gedankenwelt ist in gewissem Sinn eine beständige Flucht aus dem »Wunder.«

Ein Wunder solcher Art erlebte ich als Kind von vier oder fünf Jahren, als mir mein Vater einen Kompass zeigte. Dass diese Nadel in so bestimmter Weise sich benahm passte so gar nicht in die Art des Geschehens hinein, die in der unbewussten Begriffswelt Platz finden konnte (an »Berührung« geknüpftes Wirken). Ich erinnere mich noch jetzt–oder glaube mich zu erinnern–dass dies Erlebnis tiefen und bleibenden Eindruck auf mich gemacht hat. Da musste etwas hinter den Dingen sein, das tief verborgen war. Was der Mensch von klein auf vor sich sieht, darauf reagiert er nicht in solcher Art, er wundert sich nicht über das Fallen der Körper, über Wind und Regen, nicht über den Mond und nicht darüber, dass dieser nicht herunterfällt, nicht über die Verschiedenheit des Belebten und des Nicht-Belebten.

Im Alter von zwölf Jahren erlebte ich ein zweites Wunder ganz verschiedener Art: An einem Büchlein über Euklidische Geometrie der Ebene, das ich am Anfang eines Schuljahres in die Hand bekam. Da waren Aussagen wie z.B. das Sich-Schneiden der drei Höhen eines Dreieckes in einem Punkt, die–obwohl an sich keineswegs evident–doch mit solcher Sicherheit bewiesen werden konnten, dass ein Zweifel ausgeschlossen zu sein schien. Diese Klarheit und Sicherheit machte einen unbeschreiblichen Eindruck auf mich. Dass die Axiome unbewiesen hinzunehmen waren beunruhigte mich nicht. Überhaupt genügte es mir vollkommen, wenn ich Beweise auf solche Sätze stützen konnte, deren Gültigkeit mir nicht zweifelhaft erschien. Ich erinnere mich beispielsweise, dass mir der pythagoräische Satz von einem Onkel mitgeteilt wurde, bevor ich das heilige Geometrie-Büchlein in die Hand bekam. Nach harter Mühe gelang es mir, diesen Satz auf Grund der Ähnlichkeit von Dreiecken zu »beweisen«; dabei erschien es mir »evident,« dass die Verhältnisse der Seiten eines rechtwinkligen Dreiecks durch einen der spitzen Winkel völlig bestimmt sein müsse. Nur was nicht in

ence? This "wondering" appears to occur when an experience comes into conflict with a world of concepts already sufficiently fixed within us. Whenever such a conflict is experienced sharply and intensively it reacts back upon our world of thought in a decisive way. The development of this world of thought is in a certain sense a continuous flight from "wonder."

A wonder of this kind I experienced as a child of four or five years when my father showed me a compass. That this needle behaved in such a determined way did not at all fit into the kind of occurrences that could find a place in the unconscious world of concepts (efficacy produced by direct "touch"). I can still remember—or at least believe I can remember—that this experience made a deep and lasting impression upon me. Something deeply hidden had to be behind things. What man sees before him from infancy causes no reaction of this kind; he is not surprised by the falling of bodies, by wind and rain, nor by the moon, nor by the fact that the moon does not fall down, nor by the differences between living and nonliving matter.

At the age of twelve I experienced a second wonder of a totally different nature—in a little book dealing with Euclidean plane geometry, which came into my hands at the beginning of a school year. Here were assertions, as for example the intersection of the three altitudes of a triangle at one point, that—though by no means evident—could nevertheless be proved with such certainty that any doubt appeared to be out of the question. This lucidity and certainty made an indescribable impression upon me. That the axioms had to be accepted unproved did not disturb me. In any case it was quite sufficient for me if I could base proofs on propositions whose validity appeared to me beyond doubt. For example, I remember that an uncle told me about the Pythagorean theorem before the holy geometry booklet had come into my hands. After much effort I succeeded in "proving" this theorem on the basis of the similarity of triangles; in doing so it seemed to me "evident" that the relations of the sides of the right-angled triangles would have to be completely determined by one of the acute angles. Only whatever did not in similar fashion seem to be "evident" appeared

ähnlicher Weise ›evident‹ erschien, schien mir überhaupt eines Beweises zu bedürfen. Auch schienen mir die Gegenstände, von denen die Geometrie handelt, nicht von anderer Art zu sein als die Gegenstände der sinnlichen Wahrnehmung, ›die man sehen und greifen konnte.‹ Diese primitive Auffassung, welche wohl auch der bekannten Kant'schen Fragestellung betreffend die Möglichkeit ›synthetischer Urteile *a priori*‹ zugrundeliegt, beruht natürlich darauf, dass die Beziehung jener geometrischen Begriffe zu Gegenständen der Erfahrung (fester Stab, Strecke, usw.) unbewusst gegenwärtig war.

Wenn es so schien, dass man durch blosses Denken sichere Erkenntnis über Erfahrungsgegenstände erlangen könne, so beruhte dies ›Wunder‹ auf einem Irrtum. Aber es ist für den, der es zum ersten Mal erlebt, wunderbar genug, dass der Mensch überhaupt imstande ist, einen solchen Grad von Sicherheit und Reinheit im blossen Denken zu erlangen, wie es uns die Griechen erstmalig in der Geometrie gezeigt haben.

Nachdem ich mich nun einmal dazu habe hinreissen lassen, den notdürftig begonnenen Nekrolog zu unterbrechen, scheue ich mich nicht hier in ein paar Sätzen mein erkenntnistheoretisches Credo auszudrücken, obwohl im Vorigen einiges davon beiläufig schon gesagt ist. Dies Credo entwickelte sich erst viel später und langsam und entspricht nicht der Einstellung, die ich in jüngeren Jahren hatte.

Ich sehe auf der einen Seite die Gesamtheit der Sinnen-Erlebnisse, auf der andern Seite die Gesamtheit der Begriffe und Sätze, die in den Büchern niedergelegt sind. Die Beziehungen zwischen den Begriffen und Sätzen unter einander sind logischer Art, und das Geschäft des logischen Denkens ist strikte beschränkt auf die Herstellung der Verbindung zwischen Begriffen und Sätzen untereinander nach festgesetzten Regeln, mit denen sich die Logik beschäftigt. Die Begriffe und Sätze erhalten ›Sinn‹ bezw. ›Inhalt‹ nur durch ihre Beziehung zu Sinnen-Erlebnissen. Die Verbindung der letzteren mit den ersteren ist rein intuitiv, nicht selbst von logischer Natur. Der Grad der Sicherheit, mit der diese Beziehung bezw. intuitive Verknüpfung vorgenommen werden kann, und nichts anderes, unterscheidet die leere Phantasterei von der wissenschaftlichen ›Wahrheit.‹ Das Begriffssystem ist eine Schöpfung des Menschen samt den syntaktischen Regeln, welche die Struktur der Begriffssysteme ausmachen. Die Begriffssy-

to me to be in need of any proof at all. Also, the objects with which geometry is concerned seemed to be of no different type from the objects of sensory perception, "which can be seen and touched." This primitive conception, which probably also lies at the bottom of the well-known Kantian inquiry concerning the possibility of "synthetic judgments *a priori*," rests obviously upon the fact that the relation of geometrical concepts to objects of direct experience (rigid rod, finite interval, etc.) was unconsciously present.

If thus it appeared that it was possible to achieve certain knowledge of the objects of experience by means of pure thinking, this "wonder" rested upon an error. Nevertheless, for anyone who experiences it for the first time, it is marvelous enough that man is capable at all of reaching such a degree of certainty and purity in pure thinking as the Greeks showed us for the first time to be possible in geometry.

Now that I have allowed myself to be carried away sufficiently to interrupt my barely started obituary, I shall not hesitate to state here in a few sentences my epistemological credo, although in what precedes something has already incidentally been said about this. This credo actually evolved only much later and very slowly and does not correspond to the point of view I held in younger years.

I see on the one side the totality of sense experiences and, on the other, the totality of the concepts and propositions that are laid down in books. The relations between the concepts and propositions among themselves are of a logical nature, and the business of logical thinking is strictly limited to the achievement of the connection between concepts and propositions among themselves according to firmly laid down rules, which are the concern of logic. The concepts and propositions get "meaning," or "content," only through their connection with sense experiences. The connection of the latter with the former is purely intuitive, not itself of a logical nature. The degree of certainty with which this connection, or intuitive linkage, can be undertaken, and nothing else, differentiates empty fantasy from scientific "truth." The system of concepts is a creation of man, together with the rules of syntax, which constitute the structure of the conceptual systems. Although the conceptual

steme sind zwar an sich logisch gänzlich willkürlich, aber gebunden durch das Ziel, eine möglichst sichere (intuitive) und vollständige Zuordnung zu der Gesamtheit der Sinnen-Erlebnisse zuzulassen; zweitens erstreben sie möglichste Sparsamkeit inbezug auf ihre logisch unabhängigen Elemente (Grundbegriffe und Axiome) d.h. nicht definierte Begriffe und nicht erschlossene Sätze.

Ein Satz ist richtig, wenn er innerhalb eines logischen Systems nach den akzeptierten logischen Regeln abgeleitet ist. Ein System hat Wahrheitsgehalt, entsprechend der Sicherheit und Vollständig-keit seiner Zuordnungs-Möglichkeit zu der Erlebnis-Gesamtheit. Ein richtiger Satz erborgt seine ·Wahrheit· von dem Wahrheits-Gehalt des Systems, dem er angehört.

Eine Bemerkung zur geschichtlichen Entwicklung. Hume er-kannte klar, dass gewisse Begriffe, z.B. der der Kausalität, durch logische Methoden nicht aus dem Erfahrungsmaterial abgeleitet wer-den können. Kant, von der Unentbehrlichkeit gewisser Begriffe durchdrungen, hielt sie–so wie sie gewählt sind–für nötige Prämisse jeglichen Denkens und unterschied sie von Begriffen em-pirischen Ursprungs. Ich bin aber davon überzeugt, dass diese Unter-scheidung irrtümlich ist, bezw. dem Problem nicht in natürlicher Weise gerecht wird. Alle Begriffe, auch die erlebnis-nächsten, sind vom logischen Gesichtspunkte aus freie Setzungen, genau wie der Begriff der Kausalität, an den sich in erster Linie die Fragestellung angeschlossen hat.

Nun zurück zum Nekrolog. Im Alter von zwölf bis sechzehn machte ich mich mit den Elementen der Mathematik vertraut in-klusive der Prinzipien der Differential- und Integral-Rechnung. Dabei hatte ich das Glück auf Bücher zu stossen, die es nicht gar zu genau nahmen mit der logischen Strenge, dafür aber die Hauptgedanken übersichtlich hervortreten liessen. Diese Beschäftigung war im Ganzen wahrhaft faszinierend; es gab darin Höhepunkte, deren Ein-druck sich mit dem der elementaren Geometrie sehr wohl messen konnte–der Grundgedanke der analytischen Geometrie, die unend-lichen Reihen, der Differential- und Integral-Begriff. Auch hatte ich das Glück, die wesentlichen Ergebnisse und Methoden der gesamten Naturwissenschaft in einer vortrefflichen populären, fast durchweg aufs Qualitative sich beschränkenden Darstellung kennen zu lernen

systems are logically entirely arbitrary, they are restricted by the aim of permitting the most nearly possible certain (intuitive) and complete coordination with the totality of sense experiences; secondly they aim at the greatest possible sparsity of their logically independent elements (basic concepts and axioms), i.e., their undefined concepts and underived [postulated] propositions.

A proposition is correct if, within a logical system, it is deduced according to the accepted logical rules. A system has truth-content according to the certainty and completeness of its possibility of coordination with the totality of experience. A correct proposition borrows its "truth" from the truth-content of the system to which it belongs.

A remark as to the historical development. Hume saw clearly that certain concepts, as for example that of causality, cannot be deduced from the material of experience by logical methods. Kant, thoroughly convinced of the indispensability of certain concepts, took them–just as they are selected–to be the necessary premises of any kind of thinking and distinguished them from concepts of empirical origin. I am convinced, however, that this distinction is erroneous or, at any rate, that it does not do justice to the problem in a natural way. All concepts, even those closest to experience, are from the point of view of logic freely chosen posits, just as is the concept of causality, which was the point of departure for this inquiry in the first place.

And now back to the obituary. At the age of twelve through sixteen I familiarized myself with the elements of mathematics, including the principles of differential and integral calculus. In doing so I had the good fortune of encountering books that were not too particular regarding logical rigor, but that permitted the principal ideas to stand out clearly. This occupation was, on the whole, truly fascinating; there were peaks whose impression could easily compete with that of elementary geometry–the basic idea of analytical geometry, the infinite series, the concepts of derivative and integral. I also had the good fortune of getting to know the essential results and methods of the entire field of the natural sciences in an excellent popular exposition, which limited itself

13

(Bernsteins naturwissenschaftliche Volksbücher, ein Werk von fünf oder sechs Bänden),ein Werk, das ich mit atemloser Spannung las. Auch etwas theoretische Physik hatte ich bereits studiert, als ich mit siebzehn Jahren auf das Züricher Polytechnikum kam als Student der Mathematik und Physik.

Dort hatte ich vortreffliche Lehrer (z.B. Hurwitz, Minkowski), so dass ich eigentlich eine tiefe mathematische Ausbildung hätte erlangen können. Ich aber arbeitete die meiste Zeit im physikalischen Laboratorium, fasziniert durch die direkte Berührung mit der Erfahrung. Die übrige Zeit benutzte ich hauptsächlich, um die Werke von Kirchhoff, Helmholtz, Hertz, usw. zuhause zu studieren. Dass ich die Mathematik bis zu einem gewissen Grade vernachlässigte, hatte nicht nur den Grund, dass das naturwissenschaftliche Interesse stärker war als das mathematische, sondern das folgende eigentümliche Erlebnis. Ich sah, dass die Mathematik in viele Spezialgebiete gespalten war, deren jedes diese kurze uns vergönnte Lebenszeit wegnehmen konnte. So sah ich mich in der Lage von Buridans Esel, der sich nicht für ein besonderes Bündel Heu entschliessen konnte. Dies lag offenbar daran, dass meine Intuition auf mathematischem Gebiete nicht stark genug war, um das Fundamental-Wichtige, Grundlegende sicher von dem Rest der mehr oder weniger entbehrlichen Gelehrsamkeit zu unterscheiden. Ausserdem war aber auch das Interesse für die Natur-Erkenntnis unbedingt stärker; und es wurde mir als Student nicht klar, dass der Zugang zu den tieferen prinzipiellen Erkenntnissen in der Physik an die feinsten mathematischen Methoden gebunden war. Dies dämmerte mir erst allmählich nach Jahren selbständiger wissenschaftlicher Arbeit. Freilich war auch die Physik in Spezialgebiete geteilt, deren jedes ein kurzes Arbeitsleben verschlingen konnte, ohne dass der Hunger nach tieferer Erkenntnis befriedigt wurde. Die Masse des erfahrungsmässig Gegebenen und ungenügend Verbundenen war auch hier überwältigend. Aber bald lernte ich es hier, dasjenige herauszuspüren, was in die Tiefe führen konnte, von allem Andern aber abzusehen, von dem Vielen, das den Geist ausfüllt und von dem Wesentlichen ablenkt. Der Haken dabei war freilich, dass man für die Examina all diesen Wust in sich hineinstopfen musste, ob man nun wollte oder nicht. Dieser Zwang wirkte so abschreckend, dass mir nach überstandenem

almost throughout to qualitative aspects (Bernstein's *Popular Books on Natural Science*, a work of five or six volumes), a work that I read with breathless attention. I had also already studied some theoretical physics when, at the age of seventeen, I entered the Polytechnic Institute of Zürich as a student of mathematics and physics.

There I had excellent teachers (for example, Hurwitz, Minkowski), so that I should have been able to obtain a mathematical training in depth. I worked most of the time in the physical laboratory, however, fascinated by the direct contact with experience. The balance of the time I used, in the main, in order to study at home the works of Kirchhoff, Helmholtz, Hertz, etc. The fact that I neglected mathematics to a certain extent had its cause not merely in my stronger interest in the natural sciences than in mathematics but also in the following peculiar experience. I saw that mathematics was split up into numerous specialties, each of which could easily absorb the short lifetime granted to us. Consequently, I saw myself in the position of Buridan's ass, which was unable to decide upon any particular bundle of hay. Presumably this was because my intuition was not strong enough in the field of mathematics to differentiate clearly the fundamentally important, that which is really basic, from the rest of the more or less dispensable erudition. Also, my interest in the study of nature was no doubt stronger; and it was not clear to me as a young student that access to a more profound knowledge of the basic principles of physics depends on the most intricate mathematical methods. This dawned upon me only gradually after years of independent scientific work. True enough, physics also was divided into separate fields, each of which was capable of devouring a short lifetime of work without having satisfied the hunger for deeper knowledge. The mass of insufficiently connected experimental data was overwhelming here also. In this field, however, I soon learned to scent out that which might lead to fundamentals and to turn aside from everything else, from the multitude of things that clutter up the mind and divert it from the essentials. The hitch in this was, of course, that one had to cram all this stuff into one's mind for the examinations, whether one liked it or not. This coercion had such a deterring effect [upon me] that,

Physik, war das Werk des neunzehnten Jahrhunderts. Was aber auf den Studenten den grössten Eindruck machte, war weniger der technische Aufbau der Mechanik und die Lösung komplizierter Probleme, sondern die Leistungen der Mechanik auf Gebieten, die dem Anscheine nach nichts mit Mechanik zu tun hatten: die mechanische Lichttheorie, die das Licht als Wellenbewegung eines quasistarren elastischen Äthers auffasste, vor allem aber die kinetische Gastheorie:–Die Unabhängigkeit der spezifischen Wärme einatomiger Gase vom Atomgewicht, die Ableitung der Gasgleichung und deren Beziehung zur spezifischen Wärme, die kinetische Theorie der Dissoziation der Gase, vor allem aber der quantitative Zusammenhang von Viskosität, Wärmeleitung und Diffusion der Gase, welche auch die absolute Grösse des Atoms lieferte. Diese Ergebnisse stützten gleichzeitig die Mechanik als Grundlage der Physik und der Atomhypothese welch letztere ja in der Chemie schon fest verankert war. In der Chemie spielten aber nur die Verhältnisse der Atommassen eine Rolle, nicht deren absolute Grössen, sodass die Atomtheorie mehr als veranschaulichendes Gleichnis denn als Erkenntnis über den faktischen Bau der Materie betrachtet werden konnte. Abgesehen davon war es auch von tiefem Interesse, dass die statistische Theorie der klassischen Mechanik imstande war, die Grundgesetze der Thermodynamik zu deduzieren, was dem Wesen nach schon von Boltzmann geleistet wurde.

Wir dürfen uns daher nicht wundern, dass sozusagen alle Physiker des letzten Jahrhunderts in der klassischen Mechanik eine feste und endgültige Grundlage der ganzen Physik, ja der ganzen Naturwissenschaft sahen, und dass sie nicht müde wurden zu versuchen, auch die indessen langsam sich durchsetzende Maxwell'sche Theorie des Elektromagnetismus auf die Mechanik zu gründen. Auch Maxwell und H. Hertz, die im Rückblick mit Recht als diejenigen erscheinen, die das Vertrauen auf die Mechanik als die endgültige Basis alles physikalischen Denkens erschüttert haben, haben in ihrem bewussten Denken durchaus an der Mechanik als gesicherter Basis der Physik festgehalten. Ernst Mach war es, der in seiner *Geschichte der Mechanik* an diesem dogmatischen Glauben rüttelte; dies Buch hat gerade in dieser Beziehung einen tiefen Einfluss auf mich als Student ausgeübt. Ich sehe Machs wahre Grösse in der unbestechlichen Skepsis

masses, as the basis of all physics, was the achievement of the nineteenth century. What made the greatest impression upon the student, however, was not so much the technical development of mechanics or the solution of complicated problems as the achievements of mechanics in areas that apparently had nothing to do with mechanics: the mechanical theory of light, which conceived of light as the wave motion of a quasi-rigid elastic ether; and above all the kinetic theory of gases: the independence of the specific heat of monatomic gases from the atomic weight, the derivation of the equation of the state of a gas and its relation to the specific heat, the kinetic theory of the dissociation of gases, and above all the quantitative relationship between viscosity, heat conduction, and diffusion of gases, which also furnished the absolute magnitude of the atom. These results supported at the same time mechanics as the foundation of physics and of the atomic hypothesis, which latter was already firmly rooted in chemistry. In chemistry, however, only the ratios of the atomic masses played any role, not their absolute magnitudes, so that atomic theory could be viewed more as a visualizing symbol than as knowledge concerning the actual composition of matter. Apart from this it was also of profound interest that the statistical theory of classical mechanics was able to deduce the basic laws of thermodynamics, something in essence already accomplished by Boltzmann.

We must not be surprised, therefore, that, so to speak, all physicists of the previous century saw in classical mechanics a firm and definitive foundation for all physics, indeed for the whole of natural science, and that they never grew tired in their attempts to base Maxwell's theory of electromagnetism, which, in the meantime, was slowly beginning to win out, upon mechanics as well. Even Maxwell and H. Hertz, who in retrospect are properly recognized as those who shook the faith in mechanics as the final basis of all physical thinking, in their conscious thinking consistently held fast to mechanics as the confirmed basis of physics. It was Ernst Mach who, in his *History of Mechanics,* upset this dogmatic faith; this book exercised a profound influence upon me in this regard while I was a student. I see Mach's greatness in his incorruptible skepticism and independence; in my younger years, how-

und Unabhängigkeit; in meinen jungen Jahren hat mich aber auch Machs erkenntnistheoretische Einstellung sehr beeindruckt, die mir heute als im Wesentlichen unhaltbar erscheint, Er hat nämlich die dem Wesen nach konstruktive und spekulative Natur alles Denkens und im Besonderen des wissenschaftlichen Denkens nicht richtig ins Licht gestellt und infolge davon die Theorie gerade an solchen Stellen verurteilt, an welchen der konstruktiv-spekulative Charakter unverhüllbar zutage tritt, z.B. in der kinetischen Atomtheorie.

Bevor ich nun eingehe auf eine Kritik der Mechanik als Grundlage der Physik, muss erst etwas Allgemeines über die Gesichtspunkte gesagt werden, nach denen physikalische Theorien überhaupt kritisiert werden können. Der erste Gesichtspunkt liegt auf der Hand: die Theorie darf Erfahrungstatsachen nicht widersprechen. So einleuchtend diese Forderung auch zunächst erscheint, so subtil gestaltet sich ihre Anwendung. Man kann nämlich häufig, vielleicht sogar immer, an einer allgemeinen theoretischen Grundlage festhalten, indem man durch künstliche zusätzliche Annahmen ihre Anpassung an die Tatsachen möglich macht. Jedenfalls aber hat es dieser erste Gesichtspunkt mit der Bewährung der theoretischen Grundlage an einem vorliegenden Erfahrungsmaterial zu tun.

Der zweite Gesichtspunkt hat es nicht zu schaffen mit der Beziehung zu dem Beobachtungsmaterial sondern mit den Prämissen der Theorie selbst, mit dem, was man kurz aber undeutlich als »Natürlichkeit« oder »logische Einfachheit« der Prämissen (der Grundbegriffe und zugrunde gelegten Beziehungen zwischen diesen) bezeichnen kann. Dieser Gesichtspunkt, dessen exakte Formulierung auf grosse Schwierigkeiten stösst, hat von jeher bei der Wahl und Wertung der Theorien eine wichtige Rolle gespielt. Es handelt sich dabei nicht einfach um eine Art Abzählung der logisch unabhängigen Prämissen (wenn eine solche überhaupt eindeutig möglich wäre) sondern um eine Art gegenseitiger Abwägung inkommensurabler Qualitäten. Ferner ist von Theorien mit gleich »einfacher« Grundlage diejenige als die Überlegene zu betrachten, welche die an sich möglichen Qualitäten von Systemen am stärksten einschränkt (d.h. die bestimmtesten Aussagen enthält). Von dem »Bereich« der Theorien brauche ich hier nichts zu sagen, da wir uns auf solche Theorien beschränken, deren Gegenstand die *Gesamtheit* der physikalischen Er-

ever, Mach's epistemological position also influenced me very greatly, a position that today appears to me to be essentially untenable. For he did not place in the correct light the essentially constructive and speculative nature of all thinking and more especially of scientific thinking; in consequence, he condemned theory precisely at those points where its constructive-speculative character comes to light unmistakably, such as in the kinetic theory of atoms.

Before I enter upon a critique of mechanics as the foundation of physics, something general will have to be said first about the points of view from which physical theories may be analyzed critically at all. The first point of view is obvious: the theory must not contradict empirical facts. However evident this demand may in the first place appear, its application turns out to be quite delicate. For it is often, perhaps even always, possible to retain a general theoretical foundation by adapting it to the facts by means of artificial additional assumptions. In any case, however, this first point of view is concerned with the confirmation of the theoretical foundation by the available empirical facts.

The second point of view is not concerned with the relationship to the observations but with the premises of the theory itself, with what may briefly but vaguely be characterized as the "naturalness" or "logical simplicity" of the premises (the basic concepts and the relations between these). This point of view, whose exact formulation meets with great difficulties, has played an important role in the selection and evaluation of theories from time immemorial. The problem here is not simply one of a kind of enumeration of the logically independent premises (if anything like this were at all possible without ambiguity), but one of a kind of reciprocal weighing of incommensurable qualities. Furthermore, among theories with equally "simple" foundations, that one is to be taken as superior which most sharply delimits the otherwise feasible qualities of systems (i.e., contains the most specific claims). Of the "scope" of theories I need not speak here, inasmuch as we are confining ourselves to such theories as have for their object the *totality* of all physical phenomena. The second point of view may briefly be

den Glauben an die Möglichkeit zu verlassen, dass die gesamte Physik auf Newtons Mechanik gegründet werden könne, war die Faraday-Maxwell'sche Elektrodynamik. Diese Theorie und ihre Bestätigung durch die Hertz'schen Versuche zeigten nämlich, dass es elektromagnetische Vorgänge gibt, die ihrem Wesen nach losgelöst sind von jeglicher ponderabeln Materie – die aus elektromagnetischen »Feldern« im leeren Raume bestehenden Wellen. Wollte man die Mechanik als Grundlage der Physik aufrecht halten, so mussten die Maxwell'schen Gleichungen mechanisch interpretiert werden. Dies wurde eifrigst aber erfolglos versucht, während sich die Gleichungen in steigendem Masse als fruchtbar erwiesen. Man gewöhnte sich daran, mit diesen Feldern als selbständigen Wesenheiten zu operieren, ohne dass man sich über ihre mechanische Natur auszuweisen brauchte; so verliess man halb unvermerkt die Mechanik als Basis der Physik, weil deren Anpassung an die Tatsachen sich schliesslich als hoffnungslos darstellte. Seitdem gibt es zweierlei Begriffselemente, einerseits materielle Punkte mit Fernkräften zwischen ihnen, andererseits das kontinuierliche Feld. Es ist ein Zwischenzustand der Physik ohne einheitliche Basis für das Ganze, der – obwohl unbefriedigend – doch weit davon entfernt ist überwunden zu sein.

Nun einiges zur Kritik der Mechanik als Grundlage der Physik vom zweiten, dem inneren Gesichtspunkte aus. Solche Kritik hat bei dem heutigen Stande der Wissenschaft, d.h. nach dem Verlassen des mechanischen Fundamentes, nur noch methodisches Interesse. Sie ist aber recht geeignet eine Art des Argumentierens zu zeigen, die in der Zukunft bei der Auswahl der Theorien eine umso grössere Rolle spielen muss, je weiter sich die Grundbegriffe und Axiome von dem direkt Wahrnehmbaren entfernen, sodass das Konfrontieren der Implikationen der Theorie mit den Tatsachen immer schwieriger und langwieriger wird. Da ist in erster Linie das Mach'sche Argument zu erwähnen, das übrigens von Newton schon ganz deutlich erkannt worden war (Eimer Versuch). Alle »starren« Koordinationssysteme sind vom Standpunkt der rein geometrischen Beschreibung unter einander logisch gleichwertig. Die Gleichungen der Mechanik (z.B. schon das Trägheits-Gesetz) beanspruchen Gültigkeit nur gegenüber einer besonderen Klasse solcher Systeme, nämlich gegenüber

long time, their faith in the possibility that all physics could be founded upon Newton's mechanics, was the electrodynamics of Faraday and Maxwell. For this theory and its confirmation by Hertz's experiments showed that there are electromagnetic phenomena that by their very nature are detached from all ponderable matter –namely the waves in empty space that consist of electromagnetic "fields." If mechanics was to be maintained as the foundation of physics, Maxwell's equations had to be interpreted mechanically. This was zealously but fruitlessly attempted, whereas the equations themselves turned out to be increasingly fruitful. One got used to operating with these fields as independent substances without finding it necessary to account for their mechanical nature; thus mechanics as the basis of physics was being abandoned, almost imperceptibly, because its adaptation to the facts presented itself finally as a hopeless task. Since then, there exist two types of conceptual elements: on the one hand, material points with forces at a distance between them and, on the other hand, the continuous field. We are at an intermediate state of physics without a uniform basis for the whole, a state that–although unsatisfactory–is far from having been overcome.

Now for a few remarks concerning the critique of mechanics as the foundation of physics from the second, the "interior," point of view. In today's state of science, i.e., after the abandonment of the mechanical foundation, such a critique retains only a methodological relevance. But such a critique is well suited to show the type of argumentation that, in the selection of theories in the future, will have to play an ever greater role the more the basic concepts and axioms are removed from what is directly observable, so that the confrontation of the implications of theory by the facts becomes constantly more difficult and more drawn out. First in line to be mentioned is Mach's argument, which, incidentally, had already been clearly recognized by Newton (bucket experiment). From the standpoint of purely geometrical description, all "rigid" coordinate systems are logically equivalent. The equations of mechanics (for example the law of inertia) claim validity only when referred to a specific class of such systems, i.e., the "inertial systems." In this

den »Inertialsystemen.« Das Koordinationssystem als körperliches Objekt ist hierbei ohne Bedeutung. Man muss also für die Notwendigkeit dieser besonderen Wahl etwas suchen, was ausserhalb der Gegenstände (Massen, Abstände) liegt, von denen die Theorie handelt. Newton führte als ursächlich bestimmend deshalb ganz explicite den »absoluten Raum« ein als allgegenwärtigen aktiven Teilnehmer bei allen mechanischen Vorgängen; unter »absolut« versteht er offenbar unbeeinflusst von den Massen und ihren Bewegungen. Was den Tatbestand besonders hässlich erscheinen lässt, ist die Tatsache, dass es unendlich viele, gegen einander gleichförmig und rotationsfrei bewegte Inertialsysteme geben soll, die gegenüber allen andern starren Systemen ausgezeichnet sein sollen.

Mach vermutet, dass in einer wirklich vernünftigen Theorie die Trägheit, genau wie bei Newton die übrigen Kräfte, auf Wechselwirkung der Massen beruhen müsse, eine Auffassung die ich lange für im Prinzip die richtige hielt. Sie setzt aber implicite voraus, dass die basische Theorie eine solche vom allgemeinen Typus der Newton'schen Mechanik sein solle: Massen und Wirkungen zwischen diesen als ursprüngliche Begriffe. In eine konsequente Feldtheorie passt ein solcher Lösungsversuch nicht hinein, wie man unmittelbar einsieht.

Wie stichhaltig die Mach'sche Kritik aber an sich ist, kann man besonders deutlich aus folgender Analogie ersehen. Wir denken uns Leute, die eine Mechanik aufstellen, nur ein kleines Stück der Erdoberfläche kennen und auch keine Sterne wahrnehmen können. Sie werden geneigt sein, der vertikalen Dimension des Raumes besondere physikalische Eigenschaften zuzuschreiben (Richtung der Fallbeschleunigung) und auf Grund einer solchen begrifflichen Basis es begründen, dass der Erdboden überwiegend horizontal ist. Sie mögen sich nicht durch das Argument beeinflussen lassen, dass bezüglich der geometrischen Eigenschaften der Raum isotrop ist, und dass es daher unbefriedigend sei, physikalische Grundgesetze aufzustellen, gemäss welchen es eine Vorzugsrichtung geben soll; sie werden wohl geneigt sein (analog zu Newton) zu erklären, die Vertikale sei absolut, das zeige eben die Erfahrung und man müsse sich damit abfinden. Die Bevorzugung der Vertikalen gegen alle anderen Raum-Richtungen ist genau analog der Bevorzugung der Inertialsysteme gegen andere starre Koordinationssysteme.

connection the coordinate system as a material object is without any significance. Hence to justify the need for this specific choice one must search for something that exists beyond the objects (masses, distances) with which the theory deals. For this reason "absolute space" as originally determinative was quite explicitly introduced by Newton as the omnipresent active participant in all mechanical events; by "absolute" he obviously means: uninfluenced by the masses and by their motion. What makes this state of affairs appear particularly ugly is the fact that there are supposed to be infinitely many inertial systems, relative to each other in uniform and irrotational translation, which are supposed to be distinguished among all other rigid systems.

Mach conjectures that in a truly reasonable theory inertia would have to depend upon the interaction of the masses, precisely as was true for Newton's other forces, a conception that for a long time I considered in principle the correct one. It presupposes implicitly, however, that the basic theory should be of the general type of Newton's mechanics: masses and their interaction as the original concepts. Such an attempt at a resolution does not fit into a consistent field theory, as will be immediately recognized.

How sound, however, Mach's critique is in essence can be seen particularly clearly from the following analogy. Let us imagine people who construct a mechanics, who know only a very small part of the earth's surface and who also cannot see any stars. They will be inclined to ascribe special physical attributes to the vertical dimension of space (direction of the acceleration of falling bodies) and, on the ground of such a conceptual basis, will offer reasons that the earth is in most places horizontal. They might not let themselves be influenced by the argument that in its geometrical properties space is isotropic and that it is therefore unsatisfactory to postulate basic physical laws according to which there is to be a preferential direction; they will probably be inclined (analogously to Newton) to assert the absoluteness of the vertical, as proved by experience, as something with which one simply would have to come to terms. The preference given to the vertical over all other spatial directions is precisely analogous to the preference given to inertial systems over other rigid coordinate systems.

Nun zu anderen Argumenten die sich ebenfalls auf die innere Einfachheit bezw. Natürlichkeit der Mechanik beziehen. Wenn man die Begriffe Raum (inklusive Geometrie) und Zeit ohne kritischen Zweifel hinnimmt, so besteht an sich kein Grund, die Zugrundelegung von Fernkräften zu beanstanden, wenn ein solcher Begriff auch nicht zu denjenigen Ideen passt, die man sich auf Grund der rohen Erfahrung des Alltags bildet. Dagegen gibt es eine andere Überlegung, welche die Mechanik als Basis der Physik aufgefasst als primitiv erscheinen lässt. Es gibt im Wesentlichen zwei Gesetze

(1) das Bewegungsgesetz
(2) den Ausdruck für die Kraft bezw. die potentielle Energie.

Das Bewegungsgesetz ist präzis, aber leer, solange der Ausdruck für die Kräfte nicht gegeben ist. Für die Setzung der letzteren besteht aber ein weiter Spielraum für Willkür, besonders wenn man die an sich nicht natürliche Forderung fallen lässt, dass die Kräfte von den Koordinaten allein (und z.B. nicht von deren Differentialquotienten nach der Zeit) abhängen. Im Rahmen der Theorie ist es an sich ganz willkürlich, dass die von einem Punkte ausgehenden Gravitations- (und elektrischen) Kraftwirkungen durch die Potentialfunktion $(1/r)$ beherrscht werden. Zusätzliche Bemerkung: es ist schon lange bekannt, dass diese Funktion die zentralsymmetrische Lösung der einfachsten (drehungs-invarianten) Differentialgleichung $\Delta \varphi = 0$ ist; es wäre also naheliegend gewesen, dies als ein Anzeichen dafür zu betrachten, dass man diese Funktion als durch ein Raumgesetz bestimmt anzusehen hätte, wodurch die Willkür in der Wahl des Kraftgesetzes beseitigt worden wäre. Dies ist eigentlich die erste Erkenntnis, welche eine Abkehr von der Theorie der Fernkräfte nahelegt, welche Entwicklung–durch Faraday, Maxwell und Hertz angebahnt–unter dem äusseren Druck von Erfahrungstatsachen erst später einsetzt.

Ich möchte auch als eine innere Unsymmetrie der Theorie erwähnen, dass die im Bewegungsgesetz auftretende träge Masse auch im Kraftgesetz der Gravitation, nicht aber im Ausdruck der übrigen Kraftgesetze, auftritt. Endlich möchte ich darauf hinweisen, dass die Spaltung der Energie in zwei wesensverschiedene Teile, kinetische und potentielle Energie, als unnatürlich empfunden werden muss;

Now to [a consideration of] other arguments that also concern themselves with the inner simplicity, or naturalness, of mechanics. If one accepts the concepts of space (including geometry) and time without critical doubts, then there exists no reason to object to the idea of action at a distance, even though such a concept is unsuited to the ideas one forms on the basis of the raw experience of daily life. However, there is another consideration that makes mechanics, taken as the basis of physics, appear primitive. Essentially there are two laws:

(1) the law of motion
(2) the expression for the force or the potential energy.

The law of motion is precise, although empty as long as the expression for the forces is not given. For postulating the latter, however, there is an enormous degree of arbitrariness, especially if one drops the requirement, which is not very natural in any case, that the forces depend only on the coordinates (and not, for example, on their derivatives with respect to time). Within the framework of that theory alone it is entirely arbitrary that the forces of gravitation (and electricity), which come from one point, are governed by the potential function $(1/r)$. Additional remark: it has long been known that this function is the spherically symmetric solution of the simplest (rotation-invariant) differential equation $\nabla^2 \phi = 0$; it would therefore not have been far-fetched to regard this as a clue that this function was to be considered as resulting from a spatial law, an approach that would have eliminated the arbitrariness in the force law. This is really the first insight that suggests a turning away from the theory of action at a distance, a development that—prepared by Faraday, Maxwell, and Hertz—really begins only later in response to the external pressure of experimental data.

I would also like to mention, as one internal asymmetry of this theory, that the inertial mass that occurs in the law of motion also appears in the law of the gravitational force, but not in the expressions for the other forces. Finally I would like to point to the fact that the division of energy into two essentially different parts, kinetic and potential energy, must be felt to be unnatural; H. Hertz felt this to be

dies hat H. Hertz als so störend empfunden, dass er in seinem letzten Werk versuchte, die Mechanik von dem Begriff der potentiellen Energie (d.h. der Kraft) zu befreien.

Genug davon. Newton verzeih' mir; du fandst den einzigen Weg der zu deiner Zeit für einen Menschen von höchster Denk- und Gestaltungskraft eben noch möglich war. Die Begriffe, die du schufst, sind auch jetzt noch führend in unserem physikalischen Denken, obwohl wir nun wissen, dass sie durch andere, der Sphäre der unmittelbaren Erfahrung ferner stehende ersetzt werden müssen, wenn wir ein tieferes Begreifen der Zusammenhänge anstreben.

»Soll dies ein Nekrolog sein?« mag der erstaunte Leser fragen. Im wesentlichen ja, möchte ich antworten. Denn das Wesentliche im Dasein eines Menschen von meiner Art liegt in dem *was* er denkt und *wie* er denkt, nicht in dem, was er tut oder erleidet. Also kann der Nekrolog sich in der Hauptsache auf Mitteilung von Gedanken beschränken, die in meinem Streben eine erhebliche Rolle spielten. Eine Theorie ist desto eindrucksvoller, je grösser die Einfachheit ihrer Prämissen ist, je verschiedenartigere Dinge sie verknüpft, und je weiter ihr Anwendungsbereich ist. Deshalb der tiefe Eindruck, den die klassische Thermodynamik auf mich machte. Es ist die einzige physikalische Theorie allgemeinen Inhaltes, von der ich überzeugt bin, dass sie im Rahmen der Anwendbarkeit ihrer Grundbegriffe niemals umgestossen werden wird (zur besonderen Beachtung der grundsätzlichen Skeptiker).

Der faszinierendste Gegenstand zur Zeit meines Studiums war die Maxwell'sche Theorie. Was sie als revolutionär erscheinen liess, war der Übergang von den Fernwirkungskräften zu Feldern als Fundamentalgrössen. Die Einordnung der Optik in die Theorie des Elektromagnetismus mit ihrer Beziehung der Lichtgeschwindigkeit zum elektrischen und magnetischen absoluten Masssystem sowie die Beziehung des Brechungsexponenten zur Dielektrizitätskonstante, die qualitative zwischen Reflexionsfähigkeit und metallischer Leitfähigkeit des Körpers – es war wie eine Offenbarung. Abgesehen vom Übergang zur Feldtheorie, d.h. des Ausdrucks der elementaren Gesetze durch Differentialgleichungen, hatte Maxwell nur einen einzigen hypothetischen Schritt nötig – die Einführung des elektrischen Ver-

so disturbing that, in his very last work, he attempted to free mechanics from the concept of potential energy (i.e., from the concept of force).

Enough of this. Newton, forgive me; you found just about the only way possible in your age for a man of highest reasoning and creative power. The concepts that you created are even today still guiding our thinking in physics, although we now know that they will have to be replaced by others farther removed from the sphere of immediate experience, if we aim at a profounder understanding of relationships.

"Is this supposed to be an obituary?" the astonished reader will likely ask. I would like to reply: essentially yes. For the essential in the being of a man of my type lies precisely in *what* he thinks and *how* he thinks, not in what he does or suffers. Consequently, the obituary can limit itself in the main to the communicating of thoughts that have played a considerable role in my endeavors. A theory is the more impressive the greater the simplicity of its premises, the more different kinds of things it relates, and the more extended its area of applicability. Hence the deep impression that classical thermodynamics made upon me. It is the only physical theory of universal content concerning which I am convinced that, within the framework of the applicability of its basic concepts, it will never be overthrown (for the special attention of those who are skeptics on principle).

The most fascinating subject at the time that I was a student was Maxwell's theory. What made this theory appear revolutionary was the transition from action at a distance to fields as the fundamental variables. The incorporation of optics into the theory of electromagnetism, with its relation of the speed of light to the electric and magnetic absolute system of units as well as the relation of the index of refraction to the dielectric constant, the qualitative relation between the reflection coefficient of a body and its metallic conductivity—it was like a revelation. Aside from the transition to field theory, i.e., the expression of the elementary laws through differential equations, Maxwell needed only one single hypothetical step –the introduction of the electrical displacement current in the

schiebungsstromes im Vacuum und in den Dielektrica und seiner magnetischen Wirkung, eine Neuerung, die durch die formalen Eigenschaften der Differentialgleichungen beinahe vorgeschrieben war. In diesem Zusammenhang kann ich die Bemerkung nicht unterdrücken, dass das Paar Faraday-Maxwell so merkwürdige innere Ähnlichkeit hat mit dem Paar Galileo-Newton–der erste jedes Paares die Zusammenhänge intuitiv erfassend, der zweite sie exakt formulierend und quantitativ anwendend.

Was die Einsicht in das Wesen der elektromagnetischen Theorie zu jener Zeit erschwerte, war folgender eigentümlicher Umstand. Elektrische bezw. magnetische »Feldstärken« und »Verschiebungen« wurden als gleich elementare Grössen behandelt, der leere Raum als Spezialfall eines dielektrischen Körpers. Die *Materie* erschien als Träger des Feldes, nicht der *Raum*. Dadurch war impliziert, dass der Träger des Feldes einen Geschwindigkeitszustand besitze, und dies sollte natürlich auch vom »Vacuum« gelten (Äther). Hertz' Elektrodynamik bewegter Körper ist ganz auf diese grundsätzliche Einstellung gegründet.

Es war das grosse Verdienst von H. A. Lorentz, dass er hier in überzeugender Weise Wandel schuf. Im Prinzip gibt es nach ihm ein Feld nur im leeren Raume. Die atomistisch gedachte Materie ist einziger Sitz der elektrischen Ladungen; zwischen den materiellen Teilchen ist leerer Raum, der Sitz des elektromagnetischen Feldes, das erzeugt ist durch die Lage und Geschwindigkeit der auf den materiellen Teilchen sitzenden punktartigen Ladungen. Dielektrizität, Leitungsfähigkeit, usw. sind ausschliesslich durch die Art der mechanischen Bindung der Teilchen bedingt, aus welchen die Körper bestehen. Die Teilchen-Ladungen erzeugen das Feld, das andererseits Kräfte auf die Ladungen der Teilchen ausübt, die Bewegungen des letzteren gemäss Newtons Bewegungsgesetz bestimmend. Vergleicht man dies mit Newtons System, so besteht die Änderung darin: Die Fernkräfte werden ersetzt durch das Feld, welches auch die Strahlung mitbeschreibt. Die Gravitation wird meist ihrer relativen Kleinheit wegen unberücksichtigt gelassen; ihre Berücksichtigung war aber stets möglich durch Bereicherung der Feldstruktur, bezw. Erweiterung des Maxwell'schen Feldgesetzes. Der Physiker der gegenwärtigen Generation betrachtet den von Lorentz errungenen Standpunkt als den einzig

vacuum and in the dielectrica and its magnetic effect, an innovation that was almost preordained by the formal properties of the differential equations. In this connection I cannot suppress the remark that the pair Faraday-Maxwell has a most remarkable inner similarity with the pair Galileo-Newton – the former of each pair grasping the relations intuitively, and the second one formulating those relations exactly and applying them quantitatively.

What rendered the insight into the essence of electromagnetic theory so much more difficult at that time was the following peculiar situation. Electric or magnetic "field intensities" and "displacements" were treated as equally elementary variables, empty space as a special instance of a dielectric body. *Matter* appeared as the bearer of the field, not *space*. By this it was implied that the carrier of the field should have velocity, and this was naturally to apply to the "vacuum" (ether) also. Hertz's electrodynamics of moving bodies rests entirely upon this fundamental attitude.

It was the great merit of H. A. Lorentz that he brought about a change here in a convincing fashion. In principle a field exists, according to him, only in empty space. Matter – considered to consist of atoms – is the only seat of electric charges; between the material particles there is empty space, the seat of the electromagnetic field, which is produced by the position and velocity of the point charges located on the material particles. Dielectric behavior, conductivity, etc., are determined exclusively by the type of mechanical bindings between the particles that constitute the bodies. The particle charges create the field, which, on the other hand, exerts forces upon the charges of the particles, thus determining the motion of the latter according to Newton's law of motion. If one compares this with Newton's system, the change consists in this: action at a distance is replaced by the field, which also describes the radiation. Gravitation is usually not taken into account because of its relative smallness; its inclusion, however, was always possible by enriching the structure of the field, that is to say, by expanding Maxwell's field laws. The physicist of the present generation regards the point of view achieved by Lorentz as the only possible one; at that time,

möglichen; damals aber war es ein überraschender und kühner Schritt, ohne den die spätere Entwicklung nicht möglich gewesen wäre.

Betrachtet man diese Phase der Entwicklung der Theorie kritisch, so fällt der Dualismus auf, der darin liegt, dass materieller Punkt im Newton'schen Sinne und das Feld als Kontinuum als elementare Begriffe neben einander verwendet werden. Kinetische Energie und Feldenergie erscheinen als prinzipiell verschiedene Dinge. Dies erscheint umso unbefriedigender, als gemäss der Maxwell'schen Theorie das Magnetfeld einer bewegten elektrischen Ladung Trägheit repräsentierte. Warum also nicht die *ganze* Trägheit? Dann gäbe es nur noch Feldenergie, und das Teilchen wäre nur ein Gebiet besonders grosser Dichte der Feldenergie. Dann durfte man hoffen, den Begriff des Massenpunktes samt den Bewegungsgleichungen des Teilchens aus den Feldgleichungen abzuleiten – der störende Dualismus wäre beseitigt.

H. A. Lorentz wusste dies sehr wohl. Die Maxwell'schen Gleichungen aber erlaubten nicht, das Gleichgewicht der der ein Teilchen konstituierenden Elektrizität abzuleiten. Nur andere, *nicht lineare* Gleichungen des Feldes konnten solches vielleicht leisten. Es gab aber keine Methode, derartige Feldgleichungen herauszufinden, ohne in abenteuerliche Willkür auszuarten. Jedenfalls durfte man glauben, auf dem von Faraday und Maxwell so erfolgreich begonnenen Wege nach und nach eine neue, sichere Grundlage für die gesamte Physik zu finden.

Die durch die Einführung des Feldes begonnene Revolution war demnach keineswegs beendet. Da ereignete es sich, dass um die Jahrhundertwende unabhängig hiervon eine zweite fundamentale Krise einsetzte, deren Ernst durch Max Plancks Untersuchungen über die Wärmestrahlung (1900) plötzlich ins Bewusstsein trat. Die Geschichte dieses Geschehens ist umso merkwürdiger, weil sie wenigstens in ihrer ersten Phase nicht von irgend welchen überraschenden Entdeckungen experimenteller Art beeinflusst wurde.

Kirchhoff hatte auf thermodynamischer Grundlage geschlossen, dass die Energiedichte und spektrale Zusammensetzung der Strahlung in einem von undurchlässigen Wänden von der Temperatur T umschlossenen Hohlraum unabhängig sei von der Natur der Wände.

however, it was a surprising and audacious step, without which the later development would not have been possible.

If one views this phase of the development of theory critically, one is struck by the dualism that lies in the fact that the material point in Newton's sense and the field as continuum are used as elementary concepts side by side. Kinetic energy and field energy appear as essentially different things. This appears all the more unsatisfactory as, according to Maxwell's theory, the magnetic field of a moving electric charge represents inertia. Why not then the *whole* of inertia? Then only field energy would be left, and the particle would be merely a domain containing an especially high density of field energy. In that case one could hope to deduce the concept of the mass point together with the equations of motion of the particles from the field equations—the disturbing dualism would have been removed.

H. A. Lorentz knew this very well. However, Maxwell's equations did not permit the derivation of the equilibrium of the electricity that constitutes a particle. Only different, nonlinear field equations could possibly accomplish such a thing. But no method existed for discovering such field equations without deteriorating into adventurous arbitrariness. In any case, one could believe that it would be possible by and by to find a new and secure foundation for all of physics upon the path so successfully initiated by Faraday and Maxwell.

Accordingly, the revolution begun by the introduction of the field was by no means finished. Then it happened that, around the turn of the century, independently of what we have just been discussing, a second fundamental crisis set in, the seriousness of which was suddenly recognized owing to Max Planck's investigations into heat radiation (1900). The history of this event is all the more remarkable because, at least in its first phase, it was not in any way influenced by any surprising discoveries of an experimental nature.

On thermodynamic grounds Kirchhoff had concluded that the energy density and the spectral composition of radiation in a cavity enclosed by impervious walls of the temperature T, must be independent of the nature of the walls. That is to say, the monochromatic

35

Das heisst die nonchromatische Strahlungsdichte ρ ist eine universelle Funktion der Frequenz ν und der absoluten Temperatur T. Damit entstand das interessante Problem der Bestimmung dieser Funktion $\rho(\nu, T)$. Was konnte auf theoretischem Wege über diese Funktion ermittelt werden? Nach Maxwells Theorie musste die Strahlung auf die Wände einen durch die totale Energiedichte bestimmten Druck ausüben. Hieraus folgerte Boltzmann auf rein thermodynamischem Wege, dass die gesamte Energiedichte der Strahlung ($\int \rho \, d\nu$) proportional T^4 sei. Er fand so eine theoretische Begründung einer bereits vorher von Stefan empirisch gefundenen Gesetzmässigkeit, bezw. er verknüpfte sie mit dem Fundament der Maxwell'schen Theorie. Hierauf fand W. Wien durch eine geistvolle thermodynamische Überlegung, die ebenfalls von der Maxwell'schen Theorie Gebrauch machte, dass die universelle Funktion ρ der beiden Variabeln ν und T von der Form sein müsse

$$\rho \approx \nu^3 f\left(\frac{\nu}{T}\right),$$

wobei $f(\nu/T)$ eine universelle Funktion der einzigen Variable ν/T bedeutet. Es war klar, dass die theoretische Bestimmung dieser universellen Funktion f von fundamentaler Bedeutung war–dies war eben die Aufgabe, vor welcher Planck stand. Sorgfältige Messungen hatten zu einer recht genauen empirischen Bestimmung der Funktion f geführt. Es gelang ihm zunächst, gestützt auf diese empirischen Messungen, eine Darstellung zu finden, welche die Messungen recht gut wiedergab:

$$\rho = \frac{8\pi h\nu^3}{c^3} \frac{1}{exp(h\nu/kT) - 1}$$

wobei h und k zwei universelle Konstante sind, deren erste zur Quanten-Theorie führte. Diese Formel sieht wegen des Nenners etwas sonderbar aus. War sie auf theoretischem Wege begründbar? Planck fand tatsächlich eine Begründung, deren Unvollkommenheiten zunächst verborgen blieben, welch letzterer Umstand ein wahres Glück war für die Entwicklung der Physik. War diese Formel richtig, so erlaubte sie mit Hilfe der Maxwell'schen Theorie die Berechnung

density of radiation ρ is a universal function of the frequency v and of the absolute temperature T. Thus arose the interesting problem of determing this function $\rho(v,T)$. What could theoretically be ascertained about this function? According to Maxwell's theory the radiation had to exert a pressure on the walls, determined by the total energy density. From this Boltzmann concluded, by means of pure thermodynamics, that the entire energy density of the radiation ($\int \rho \, dv$) is proportional to T^4. In this way he found a theoretical justification of a law that had previously been discovered empirically by Stefan; i.e., in this way he connected this empirical law with the basis of Maxwell's theory. Thereafter, by way of an ingenious thermodynamic consideration, which also made use of Maxwell's theory, W. Wien found that the universal function ρ of the two variables v and T would have to be of the form

$$\rho \approx v^3 f\left(\frac{v}{T}\right),$$

whereby $f(v/T)$ is a universal function of the one variable v/T. It was clear that the theoretical determination of this universal function f was of fundamental importance–this was precisely the task that confronted Planck. Careful measurements had led to a rather precise empirical determination of the function f. Relying on those empirical measurements, he succeeded in the first place in finding a statement that rendered the measurements very well indeed:

$$\rho = \frac{8\pi h v^3}{c^3} \frac{1}{exp(hv/kT)-1}$$

whereby h and k are two universal constants, the first of which led to quantum theory. Because of the denominator, this formula looks a bit queer. Was it possible to derive it theoretically? Planck actually did find a derivation, the imperfections of which remained at first hidden, which latter fact was most fortunate for the development of physics. If this formula was correct, it permitted, with the aid of Maxwell's theory, the calculation of the average energy E

der mittleren Energie E eines in dem Strahlungsfelde befindlichen quasi-monochromatischen Oszillators:

$$E = \frac{h\nu}{exp(\,h\nu/kT)-1}\,.$$

Planck zog es vor zu versuchen, diese letztere Grösse theoretisch zu berechnen. Bei diesem Bestreben half zunächst die Thermodynamik nicht mehr, und ebensowenig die Maxwell'sche Theorie. Was nun an dieser Formel ungemein ermutigend war, war folgender Umstand. Sie lieferte für hohe Werte der Temperatur (bei festem ν) den Ausdruck

$$E = kT.$$

Es ist dies derselbe Ausdruck, den die kinetische Gastheorie für die mittlere Energie eines in einer Dimension elastisch schwingungsfähigen Massenpunktes liefert. Diese liefert nämlich

$$E = (R/N)T,$$

wobei R die Konstante der Gasgleichung und N die Anzahl der Moleküle im Grammmolekül bedeutet, welche Konstante die absolute Grösse des Atoms ausdrückt. Die Gleichsetzung beider Ausdrücke liefert

$$N = R/k.$$

Die eine Konstante der Planck'schen Formel liefert also exakt die wahre Grösse des Atoms. Der Zahlenwert stimmte befriedigend überein mit den allerdings wenig genauen Bestimmungen von N mit Hilfe der kinetischen Gastheorie.

Dies war ein grosser Erfolg, den Planck klar erkannte. Die Sache hat aber eine bedenkliche Kehrseite, die Planck zunächst glücklicher Weise übersah. Die Überlegung verlangt nämlich, dass die Beziehung $E = kT$ auch für kleine Temperaturen gelten müsse. Dann aber wäre es aus mit der Planck'schen Formel und mit der Konstante h. Die richtige Konsequenz aus der bestehenden Theorie wäre also gewesen: Die mittlere kinetische Energie des Oszillators wird entweder durch die Gastheorie falsch geliefert, was eine Widerlegung der Mechanik bedeuten würde; oder die mittlere Energie des Oszillators ergibt sich

of a quasi-monochromatic oscillator within the field of radiation:

$$E = \frac{h\nu}{exp(h\nu/kT)-1} .$$

Planck preferred to attempt calculating this latter magnitude theoretically. In this effort, thermodynamics, for the time being, no longer proved helpful, and neither did Maxwell's theory. This expression had one aspect that was most encouraging. For high temperatures (with ν fixed) it yielded the expression

$$E = kT.$$

This is the same expression obtained in the kinetic theory of gases for the average energy of a mass point capable of oscillating elastically in one dimension. For in kinetic gas theory one gets

$$E = (R/N)T,$$

where R denotes the gas constant, and N the number of molecules per mole, from which constant one can compute the absolute size of the atom. Equating these two expressions one gets

$$N = R/k.$$

The one constant of Planck's formula consequently furnishes exactly the correct size of the atom. The numerical value agreed satisfactorily with the determinations of N by means of kinetic gas theory, though the latter were not very accurate.

This was a great success, which Planck clearly recognized. But the matter has a serious drawback, which Planck fortunately overlooked at first. For the same considerations demand in fact that the relation $E = kT$ would also have to be valid for low temperatures. In that case, however, it would be all over with Planck's formula and with the constant h. From the existing theory, therefore, the correct conclusion would have been: the average kinetic energy of the oscillator is either given incorrectly by the theory of gases, which would imply a refutation of [statistical] mechanics; or else the average energy of the oscillator follows incorrectly from Maxwell's theory,

unrichtig aus der Maxwell'schen Theorie, was eine Widerlegung der letzteren bedeuten würde. Am Wahrscheinlichsten ist es unter diesen Verhältnissen, dass beide Theorien nur in der Grenze richtig, im Übrigen aber falsch sind; so verhält es sich auch in der Tat, wie wir im Folgenden sehen werden. Hätte Planck so geschlossen, so hätte er vielleicht seine grosse Entdeckung nicht gemacht, weil seiner Überlegung das Fundament entzogen worden wäre.

Nun zurück zu Planck's Überlegung. Boltzmann hatte auf Grund der kinetischen Gastheorie gefunden, dass die Entropie, abgesehen von einem konstanten Faktor, gleich dem Logarithmus der »Wahrscheinlichkeit« des ins Auge gefassten Zustandes sei. Er hat damit das Wesen der im Sinne der Thermodynamik »nicht umkehrbaren« Vorgänge erkannt. Vom molekular-mechanischen Gesichtspunkte aus gesehen sind dagegen alle Vorgänge umkehrbar. Nennt man einen molekulartheoretisch definierten Zustand einen mikroskopisch beschriebenen oder kurz Mikrozustand, einen im Sinne der Thermodynamik beschriebenen Zustand einen Makrozustand, so gehören zu einem makroskopischen Zustand ungeheuer viele (Z) Zustände. Z ist dann das Mass für die Wahrscheinlichkeit eines ins Auge gefassten Makrozustandes. Dies Idee erscheint auch darum von überragender Bedeutung, dass ihre Anwendbarkeit nicht auf die mikroskopische Beschreibung auf der Grundlage der Mechanik beschränkt ist. Dies erkannte Planck und wendete das Boltzmann'sche Prinzip auf ein System an, das aus sehr vielen Resonatoren von derselben Frequenz v besteht. Der makroskopische Zustand ist gegeben durch die Gesamtenergie der Schwingung aller Resonatoren, ein Mikrozustand durch Angabe der (momentanen) Energie jedes einzelnen Resonators. Um nun die Zahl der zu einem Makrozustand gehörigen Mikrozustände durch eine endliche Zahl ausdrücken zu können, teilte er die Gesamtenergie in eine grosse aber endliche Zahl von gleichen Energie-Elementen ξ und fragte: auf wieviele Arten können diese Energie-Elemente unter die Resonatoren verteilt werden. Der Logarithmus dieser Zahl liefert dann die Entropie und damit (auf thermodynamischem Wege) die Temperatur des Systems. Planck erhielt nun seine Strahlungsformel, wenn er seine Energie-Elemente ξ von der Grösse $\xi = hv$ wählte. Das Entscheidende dabei ist, dass das Ergebnis daran gebunden ist, dass man für ξ einen bestimmten endlichen Wert

which would imply a refutation of the latter. Under such circumstances it is most probable that both theories are correct only in the limit, but are otherwise false; this is indeed the situation, as we shall see in what follows. If Planck had drawn this conclusion, he probably would not have made his great discovery, because pure deductive reasoning would have been left without a foundation.

Now back to Planck's reasoning. On the basis of the kinetic theory of gases Boltzmann had discovered that, aside from a constant factor, entropy was equal to the logarithm of the "probability" of the state under consideration. Through this insight he recognized the nature of processes that, within the meaning of thermodynamics, are "irreversible." Seen from the molecular-mechanical point of view, however, all processes are reversible. If one calls a state defined in terms of the molecular theory a microscopically described one, or, more briefly, a micro-state, and a state described in terms of thermodynamics a macro-state, then an immensely large number (Z) of states belong to a macroscopic condition. Z then is a measure of the probability of a chosen macro-state. This idea appears to be of outstanding importance also because its applicability is not limited to a microscopic description on the basis of mechanics. Planck recognized this and applied Boltzmann's principle to a system consisting of very many resonators of the same frequency v. The macroscopic state is given by the total energy of the oscillation of all resonators, a micro-state by the fixation of the (instantaneous) energy of each individual resonator. In order to be able to express the number of micro-states belonging to a macro-state by means of a finite number, he [Planck] divided the total energy into a large but finite number of identical energy elements ξ and asked: in how many ways can these energy elements be divided among the resonators. The logarithm of this number, then, furnishes the entropy and thus (via thermodynamics) the temperature of the system. Planck got his radiation formula if he chose his energy elements ξ to have the magnitude $\xi = hv$. The decisive element in this procedure is that the result depends on taking for ξ a definite finite value, i.e., on not going

nimmt, also nicht zum Limes $\xi=0$ übergeht. Diese Form der Überlegung lässt nicht ohne Weiteres erkennen, dass dieselbe mit der
mechanischen und elektrodynamischen Basis im Widerspruch steht,
auf welcher die Ableitung im Übrigen beruht. In Wirklichkeit setzt
die Ableitung aber implicite voraus, dass die Energie nur in »Quanten«
von der Grösse hv von dem einzelnen Resonator absorbiert und
emittiert werden kann, dass also sowohl die Energie eines schwingungsfähigen mechanischen Gebildes als auch die Energie der Strahlung nur in solchen Quanten umgesetzt werden kann—im Gegensatz
mit den Gesetzen der Mechanik und Elektrodynamik. Hierbei war
der Widerspruch mit der Dynamik fundamental, während der
Widerspruch mit der Elektrodynamik weniger fundamental sein
konnte. Der Ausdruck für die Dichte der Strahlungsenergie ist nämlich zwar *vereinbar* mit den Maxwell'schen Gleichungen, aber
keine notwendige Folge dieser Gleichungen. Dass dieser Ausdruck
wichtige Mittelwerte liefert, zeigt sich ja dadurch, dass die auf ihm
beruhenden Gesetze von Stefan-Boltzmann und Wien mit der Erfahrung im Einklang sind.

All dies war mir schon kurze Zeit nach dem Erscheinen von
Plancks grundlegender Arbeit klar, sodass ich, ohne einen Ersatz für
die klassische Mechanik zu haben, doch sehen konnte, zu was für
Konsequenzen dies Gesetz der Temperaturstrahlung für den licht-
elektrischen Effekt und andere verwandte Phänomene der Verwand-
lung von Strahlungsenergie sowie für die spezifische Wärme (insbesondere) fester Körper führt. All meine Versuche, das theoretische Fundament der Physik diesen Erkenntnissen anzupassen, schei-
terten aber völlig. Es war wie wenn einem der Boden unter den
Füssen weggezogen worden wäre, ohne dass sich irgendwo fester
Grund zeigte, auf dem man hätte bauen können. Dass diese schwan-
kende und widerspruchsvolle Grundlage hinreichte um einen Mann
mit dem einzigartigen Instinkt und Feingefühl Bohrs in den Stand
zu setzen, die hauptsächlichen Gesetze der Spektrallinien und der
Elektronenhüllen der Atome nebst deren Bedeutung für die Chemie
aufzufinden, erschien mir wie ein Wunder—und erscheint mir auch
heute noch als ein Wunder. Dies ist höchste Musikalität auf dem
Gebiete des Gedankens.

Mein eigenes Interesse in jenen Jahren war weniger auf die
Einzel-Folgerungen aus dem Planck'schen Ergebnis gerichtet, so wich-

to the limit $\xi = 0$. This form of reasoning does not make obvious the fact that it contradicts the mechanical and electrodynamic basis upon which the derivation otherwise depends. Actually, however, the derivation presupposes implicitly that energy can be absorbed and emitted by the individual resonator only in "quanta" of magnitude $h\nu$, i.e., that the energy of a mechanical structure capable of oscillations as well as the energy of radiation can be transferred only in such quanta–in contradiction to the laws of mechanics and electrodynamics. The contradiction with dynamics was here fundamental; whereas the contradiction with electrodynamics might be less fundamental. For the expression for the density of radiation energy, though *compatible* with Maxwell's equations, is not a necessary consequence of these equations. That this expression furnishes important mean values is shown by the fact that the Stefan-Boltzmann law and Wien's law, which are based on it, are in agreement with experience.

All of this was quite clear to me shortly after the publication of Planck's fundamental work; so that, without having a substitute for classical mechanics, I could nevertheless see to what kind of consequences this law of temperature radiation leads for the photoelectric effect and for other related phenomena of the transformation of radiation energy, as well as for the specific heat of (especially) solid bodies. All my attempts, however, to adapt the theoretical foundation of physics to this [new type of] knowledge failed completely. It was as if the ground had been pulled out from under one, with no firm foundation to be seen anywhere upon which one could have built. That this insecure and contradictory foundation was sufficient to enable a man of Bohr's unique instinct and sensitivity to discover the principal laws of the spectral lines and of the electron shells of the atoms, together with their significance for chemistry, appeared to me as a miracle–and appears to me a miracle even today. This is the highest form of musicality in the sphere of thought.

My own interest in those years was less concerned with the detailed consequences of Planck's results, however important these

tig diese auch sein mochten. Meine Hauptfrage war: Was für allgemeine Folgerungen können aus der Strahlungsformel betreffend die Struktur der Strahlung und überhaupt betreffend das elektromagnetische Fundament der Physik gezogen werden? Bevor ich hierauf eingehe, muss ich einige Untersuchungen kurz erwähnen, die sich auf die Brown'sche Bewegung und verwandte Gegenstände (Schwankungs-Phänomene) beziehen und sich in der Hauptsache auf die klassisch Molekularmechanik gründen. Nicht vertraut mit den früher erschienen und den Gegenstand tatsächlich erschöpfenden Untersuchungen von Boltzmann und Gibbs, entwickelte ich die statistische Mechanik und die auf sie gegründete molekular-kinetische Theorie der Thermodynamik. Mein Hauptziel dabei war es, Tatsachen zu finden, welche die Existenz von Atomen von bestimmter endlicher Grösse möglichst sicher stellten. Dabei entdeckte ich, dass es nach der atomistischen Theorie eine der Beobachtung zugängliche Bewegung suspendierter mikroskopischer Teilchen geben müsse, ohne zu wissen, dass Beobachtungen über die ·Brown'sche Bewegung· schon lange bekannt waren. Die einfachste Ableitung beruhte auf folgender Erwägung. Wenn die molekular-kinetische Theorie im Prinzip richtig ist, muss eine Suspension von sichtbaren Teilchen ebenso einen die Gasgesetze erfüllenden osmotischen Druck besitzen wie eine Lösung von Molekülen. Dieser osmotische Druck hängt ab von der wahren Grösse der Moleküle, d.h. von der Zahl der Moleküle in einem Gramm-Äquivalent. Ist die Suspension von ungleichmässiger Dichte, so gibt die damit vorhandene räumliche Variabilität dieses osmotischen Druckes Anlass zu einer ausgleichenden Diffusionsbewegung, welche aus der bekannten Beweglichkeit der Teilchen berechenbar ist. Dieser Diffusionsvorgang kann aber andererseits auch aufgefasst werden als das Ergebnis der zunächst ihrem Betrage nach unbekannten regellosen Verlagerung der suspendierten Teilchen unter der Wirkung der thermischen Agitation. Durch Gleichsetzung der durch beide Überlegungen erlangten Beträge für den Diffusionsfluss erhält man quantitativ das statistische Gesetz für jene Verlagerungen, d.h. das Gesetz der Brown'schen Bewegung. Die Übereinstimmung dieser Betrachtung mit der Erfahrung zusammen mit der Planck'schen Bestimmung der wahren Molekülgrösse aus dem Strahlungsgesetz (für hohe Temperaturen) überzeugte die damals zahlreichen Skeptiker

might be. My main question was: What general conclusions can be drawn from the radiation formula concerning the structure of radiation and even more generally concerning the electromagnetic foundation of physics? Before I take this up, I must briefly mention a number of investigations that relate to the Brownian motion and related objects (fluctuation phenomena) and that in essence rest upon classical molecular mechanics. Not acquainted with the investigations of Boltzmann and Gibbs, which had appeared earlier and actually exhausted the subject, I developed the statistical mechanics and the molecular-kinetic theory of thermodynamics based upon it. My principal aim in this was to find facts that would guarantee as much as possible the existence of atoms of definite finite size. In the midst of this I discovered that, according to atomistic theory, there would have to be a movement of suspended microscopic particles capable of being observed, without knowing that observations concerning the Brownian motion were already long familiar. The simplest derivation rested upon the following consideration. If the molecular-kinetic theory is essentially correct, a suspension of visible particles must possess the same kind of osmotic pressure satisfying the gas laws as a solution of molecules. This osmotic pressure depends upon the actual magnitude of the molecules, i.e., upon the number of molecules in a gram-equivalent. If the density of the suspension is inhomogeneous, the osmotic pressure is inhomogeneous, too, and gives rise to a compensating diffusion, which can be calculated from the known mobility of the particles. This diffusion can, on the other hand, also be considered the result of the random displacement—originally of unknown magnitude–of the suspended particles owing to thermal agitation. By comparing the amounts obtained for the diffusion current from both types of reasoning, one obtains quantitatively the statistical law for those displacements, i.e., the law of the Brownian motion. The agreement of these considerations with experience together with Planck's determination of the true molecular size from the law of radiation (for high temperatures) convinced the skeptics, who were quite numerous at that time (Ostwald, Mach),

45

(Ostwald, Mach) von der Realität der Atome. Die Abneigung dieser Forscher gegen die Atomtheorie ist ohne Zweifel auf ihre positivistische philosophische Einstellung zurückzuführen. Es ist dies ein interessantes Beispiel dafür, dass selbst Forscher von kühnem Geist und von feinem Instinkt durch philosophische Vorurteile für die Interpretation von Tatsachen gehemmt werden können. Das Vorurteil –welches seither keineswegs ausgestorben ist–liegt in dem Glauben, dass die Tatsachen allein ohne freie begriffliche Konstruktion wissenschaftliche Erkenntnis liefern könnten und sollten. Solche Täuschung ist nur dadurch möglich, dass man sich der freien Wahl von solchen Begriffen nicht leicht bewusst werden kann, die durch Bewährung und langen Gebrauch unmittelbar mit dem empirischen Material verknüpft zu sein scheinen.

Der Erfolg der Theorie der Brown'schen Bewegung zeigte wieder deutlich, dass die klassische Mechanik stets dann zuverlässige Resultate lieferte, wenn sie auf Bewegungen angewandt wurde, bei welchen die höheren zeitlichen Ableitungen der Geschwindigkeit vernachlässigbar klein sind. Auf diese Erkenntnis lässt sich eine verhältnismässig direkte Methode gründen, um aus der Planck'schen Formel etwas zu erfahren über die Konstitution der Strahlung. Man darf nämlich schliessen, dass in einem Strahlungsraume ein (senkrecht zu seiner Ebene) frei bewegter, quasi-monochromatisch reflektierender Spiegel eine Art Brown'sche Bewegung ausführen muss, deren mittlere kinetische Energie gleich $1/2(R/N)T$ ist (R = Konstante der Gasgleichung für ein Gramm-Molekül, N gleich Zahl der Moleküle in einem Gramm-Molekül, T = absolute Temperatur). Wäre die Strahlung keinen lokalen Schwankungen unterworfen, so würde der Spiegel allmählich zur Ruhe kommen, weil er auf seiner Vorderseite infolge seiner Bewegung mehr Strahlung reflektiert als auf seiner Rückseite. Er muss aber gewisse aus der Maxwell'schen Theorie berechenbare unregelmässige Schwankungen des auf ihn wirkenden Druckes dadurch erfahren, dass die die Strahlung konstituierenden Wellenbündel miteinander interferieren. Diese Rechnung zeigt nun, dass diese Druckschwankungen (insbesondere bei geringen Strahlungsdichten) keineswegs hinreichen um dem Spiegel die mittlere kinetische Energie $1/2(R/N)T$ zu erteilen. Um dies Resultat zu erhalten, muss man vielmehr annehmen, dass es eine zweite aus der Maxwell'schen Theorie nicht

of the reality of atoms. The hostility of these scholars toward atomic theory can undoubtedly be traced back to their positivistic philosophical attitude. This is an interesting example of the fact that even scholars of audacious spirit and fine instinct can be hindered in the interpretation of facts by philosophical prejudices. The prejudice –which has by no means disappeared–consists in the belief that facts by themselves can and should yield scientific knowledge without free conceptual construction. Such a misconception is possible only because one does not easily become aware of the free choice of such concepts, which, through success and long usage, appear to be immediately connected with the empirical material.

The success of the theory of the Brownian motion showed again conclusively that classical mechanics always led to trustworthy results whenever it was applied to motions in which the higher time derivatives of the velocity are negligible. Upon this recognition a relatively direct method can be based that permits us to learn something concerning the constitution of radiation from Planck's formula. One may argue that in a space filled with radiation a freely moving (vertically to its plane), quasi-monochromatically reflecting mirror would have to go through a kind of Brownian movement, the mean kinetic energy of which equals $1/2(R/N)T$ (R = gas constant for one gram-molecule, N = the number of molecules per mole, T = absolute temperature). If radiation were not subject to local fluctuations, the mirror would gradually come to rest because, owing to its motion, it reflects more radiation on its front than on its reverse side. The mirror, however, must experience certain random fluctuations of the pressure exerted upon it because of the fact that the wave packets, constituting the radiation, interfere with one another. These can be computed from Maxwell's theory. This calculation, then, shows that these pressure variations (especially in the case of small radiation densities) are by no means sufficient to impart to the mirror the average kinetic energy $1/2(R/N)T$. In order to get this result one has to assume rather that there exists a second type of pressure variations, not derivable from Maxwell's theory, correspond-

folgende Art Druckschwankungen gibt, welche der Annahme entspricht, dass die Strahlungsenergie aus unteilbaren punktartig lokalisierten Quanten von der Energie $h\nu$ [und dem Impuls $h\nu/c$, ($c =$ Lichtgeschwindigkeit)] besteht, die ungeteilt reflektiert werden. Diese Betrachtung zeigte in einer drastischen und direkten Weise, dass den Planck'schen Quanten eine Art unmittelbare Realität zugeschrieben werden muss, dass also die Strahlung in energetischer Beziehung eine Art Molekularstruktur besitzen muss, was natürlich mit der Maxwell'schen Theorie im Widerspruch ist. Auch Überlegungen über die Strahlung, die unmittelbar auf Boltzmanns Entropie-Wahrscheinlichkeits-Relation gegründet sind (Wahrscheinlichkeit = statistische zeitliche Häufigkeit gesetzt) führten zu demselben Resultat. Diese Doppelnatur von Strahlung (und materiellen Korpuskeln) ist eine Haupteigenschaft der Realität, welche die Quanten-Mechanik in einer geistreichen und verblüffend erfolgreichen Weise gedeutet hat. Diese Deutung welche von fast allen zeitgenössischen Physikern als im wesentlichen endgültig angesehen wird, erscheint mir als ein nur temporärer Ausweg; einige Bemerkungen darüber folgen später.

Überlegungen solcher Art machten es mir schon kurz nach 1900, d.h. kurz nach Plancks bahnbrechender Arbeit klar, dass weder die Mechanik noch die Elektrodynamik (ausser in Grenzfällen) exakte Gültigkeit beanspruchen können. Nach und nach verzweifelte ich an der Möglichkeit die wahren Gesetze durch auf bekannte Tatsachen sich stützende konstruktive Bemühungen herauszufinden. Je länger und verzweifelter ich mich bemühte, desto mehr kam ich zu der Überzeugung, dass nur die Auffindung eines allgemeinen formalen Prinzipes uns zu gesicherten Ergebnissen führen könnte. Als Vorbild sah ich die Thermodynamik vor mir. Das allgemeine Prinzip war dort in dem Satze gegeben: die Naturgesetze sind so beschaffen, dass es unmöglich ist, ein *perpetuum mobile* (erster und zweiter Art) zu konstruieren. Wie aber ein solches allgemeines Prinzip finden? Ein solches Prinzip ergab sich nach zehn Jahren Nachdenkens aus einem Paradoxon, auf das ich schon mit sechzehn Jahren gestossen bin: Wenn ich einem Lichtstrahl nacheile mit der Geschwindigkeit c (Lichtgeschwindigkeit im Vacuum), so sollte ich einen solchen Lichtstrahl als ruhendes, räumlich oszillatorisches elektromagnetisches Feld wahr-

ing to the assumption that radiation energy consists of indivisible point-like localized quanta of energy $h\nu$ [and of momentum $h\nu/c$, (c = velocity of light)], which are reflected undivided. This way of looking at the problem showed in a drastic and direct way that a type of immediate reality has to be ascribed to Planck's quanta, that radiation must, therefore, possess a kind of molecular structure as far as its energy is concerned, which of course contradicts Maxwell's theory. Considerations about radiation based directly on Boltzmann's entropy probability relation (probability taken to equal statistical temporal frequency) also lead to the same result. This dual nature of radiation (and of material corpuscles) is a major property of reality, which has been interpreted by quantum mechanics in an ingenious and amazingly successful fashion. This interpretation, which is looked upon as essentially definitive by almost all contemporary physicists, appears to me to be only a temporary expedient; a few remarks to this [point] will follow later.

Reflections of this type made it clear to me as long ago as shortly after 1900, i.e., shortly after Planck's trailblazing work, that neither mechanics nor electrodynamics could (except in limiting cases) claim exact validity. Gradually I despaired of the possibility of discovering the true laws by means of constructive efforts based on known facts. The longer and the more desperately I tried, the more I came to the conviction that only the discovery of a universal formal principle could lead us to assured results. The example I saw before me was thermodynamics. The general principle was there given in the theorem: The laws of nature are such that it is impossible to construct a *perpetuum mobile* (of the first and second kind). How, then, could such a universal principle be found? After ten years of reflection such a principle resulted from a paradox upon which I had already hit at the age of sixteen: If I pursue a beam of light with the velocity c (velocity of light in a vacuum), I should observe such a beam of light as an electromagnetic field at rest though spatially oscillating. There seems to be no such thing, however, neither on the

nehmen. So etwas scheint es aber nicht zu geben, weder auf Grund der Erfahrung noch gemäss den Maxwell'schen Gleichungen. Intuitiv klar schien es mir von vornherein, dass von einem solchen Beobachter aus beurteilt alles sich nach denselben Gesetzen abspielen müsse wie für einen relativ zu Erde ruhenden Beobachter. Denn wie sollte der erste Beobachter wissen bezw. konstatieren können, dass er sich im Zustand rascher gleichförmiger Bewegung befindet?

Man sieht, dass in diesem Paradoxon der Keim zur speziellen Relativitätstheorie schon enthalten ist. Heute weiss natürlich jeder, dass alle Versuche, dies Paradoxon befriedigend aufzuklären, zum Scheitern verurteilt waren, solange das Axiom des absoluten Charakters der Zeit, bezw. der Gleichzeitigkeit, unerkannt im Unbewussten verankert war. Dies Axiom und seine Willkür klar erkennen bedeutet eigentlich schon die Lösung des Problems. Das kritische Denken, dessen es zur Auffindung dieses zentralen Punktes bedurfte, wurde bei mir entscheidend gefördert insbesondere durch die Lektüre von David Humes und Ernst Machs philosophischen Schriften.

Man hatte sich darüber klar zu werden, was die räumlichen Koordinaten und der Zeitwert eines Ereignisses in der Physik bedeuteten. Die physikalische Deutung der räumlichen Koordinaten setzten einen starren Bezugskörper voraus, der noch dazu von mehr oder minder bestimmtem Bewegungszustände (Inertialsystem) sein musste. Bei gegebenem Inertialsystem bedeuteten die Koordinaten Ergebnisse von bestimmten Messungen mit starren (ruhenden) Stäben. (Dass die Voraussetzung der prinzipiellen Existenz starrer Stäbe eine durch approximative Erfahrung nahe gelegte aber im Prinzip willkürliche Voraussetzung ist, dessen soll man sich stets bewusst sein.) Bei solcher Interpretation der räumlichen Koordinaten wird die Frage der Gültigkeit der Euklidischen Geometrie zum physikalischen Problem.

Sucht man nun die Zeit eines Ereignisses analog zu deuten, so braucht man ein Mittel zur Messung der Zeitdifferenz (in sich determinierter periodischer Prozess realisiert durch ein System von hinreichend geringer räumlicher Abmessung). Eine relativ zum Inertialsystem ruhend angeordnete Uhr definiert eine (Orts-Zeit). Die Orts-Zeiten aller räumlichen Punkte zusammen genommen sind die ▸Zeit,◂ die zu dem gewählten Inertialsystem gehört, wenn man noch

basis of experience nor according to Maxwell's equations. From the very beginning it appeared to me intuitively clear that, judged from the standpoint of such an observer, everything would have to happen according to the same laws as for an observer who, relative to the earth, was at rest. For how should the first observer know, or be able to determine, that he is in a state of fast uniform motion?

One sees that in this paradox the germ of the special relativity theory is already contained. Today everyone knows, of course, that all attempts to clarify this paradox satisfactorily were condemned to failure as long as the axiom of the absolute character of time, or of simultaneity, was rooted unrecognized in the unconscious. To recognize clearly this axiom and its arbitrary character already implies the essentials of the solution of the problem. The type of critical reasoning required for the discovery of this central point was decisively furthered, in my case, especially by the reading of David Hume's and Ernst Mach's philosophical writings.

One had to understand clearly what the spatial coordinates and the time fixation of an event signified in physics. The physical interpretation of the spatial coordinates presupposed a rigid body of reference, which, moreover, had to be in a more or less definite state of motion (inertial system). In a given inertial system the coordinates denoted the results of certain measurements with rigid (stationary) rods. (One should always be aware that the presupposition of the existence in principle of rigid rods is a presupposition suggested by approximate experience but is, in principle, arbitrary.) With such an interpretation of the spatial coordinates the question of the validity of Euclidean geometry becomes a problem of physics.

If, then, one tries to interpret the time of an event analogously, one needs a means for the measurement of the difference in time (a periodic process, internally determined, and realized by a system of sufficiently small spatial extension). A clock at rest relative to the system of inertia defines a local time. The local times of all space points taken together are the "time," which belongs to the selected system of inertia, if a means is given to "set" these clocks relative

ein Mittel gegeben hat, diese Uhren gegeneinander zu -richten.- Man sieht, dass es *a priori* gar nicht nötig ist, dass die in solcher Weise definierten -Zeiten- verschiedener Inertialsysteme miteinander übereinstimmen. Man würde dies längst gemerkt haben, wenn nicht für die praktische Erfahrung des Alltags (wegen des hohen Wertes von c) das Licht nicht als Mittel für die Konstatierung absoluter Gleichzeitigkeit erschiene.

Die Voraussetzung von der (prinzipiellen) Existenz (idealer bezw. vollkommener) Massstäbe und Uhren ist nicht unabhängig voneinander, denn ein Lichtsignal, welches zwischen den Enden eines starren Stabes hin und her reflektiert wird, stellt eine ideale Uhr dar, vorausgesetzt, dass die Voraussetzung von der Konstanz der Vacuum-Lichtgeschwindigkeit nicht zu Widersprüchen führt.

Das obige Paradoxon lässt sich nun so formulieren. Nach den in der klassischen Physik verwendeten Verknüpfungsregeln von räumlichen Koordinaten und Zeit von Ereignissen beim Übergang von einem Inertialsystem zu einem andern sind die beiden Annahmen

(1) Konstanz der Lichtgeschwindigkeit
(2) Unabhängigkeit der Gesetze (also speziell auch des Gesetzes von der Konstanz der Lichtgeschwindigkeit) von der Wahl des Inertialsystems (spezielles Relativitätsprinzip)

miteinander unvereinbar (trotzdem beide einzeln durch die Erfahrung gestützt sind).

Die der speziellen Rel. Th. zugrunde liegende Erkenntnis ist: Die Annahmen (1) und (2) sind miteinander vereinbar, wenn für die Umrechnung von Koordinaten und Zeiten der Ereignisse neuartige Beziehungen (-Lorentz-Transformation-) zugrunde gelegt werden. Bei der gegebenen physikalischen Interpretation von Koordinaten und Zeit bedeutet dies nicht etwa nur einen konventionellen Schritt sondern involviert bestimmte Hypothesen über das tatsächliche Verhalten bewegter Massstäbe und Uhren, die durch Experiment bestätigt bezw. widerlegt werden können.

Das allgemeine Prinzip der speziellen Relativitätstheorie ist in dem Postulat enthalten: Die Gesetze der Physik sind invariant mit Bezug auf Lorentz-Transformationen (für den Übergang von einem Inertialsystem zu einem beliebigen andern Inertialsystem). Dies ist

to each other. One sees that *a priori* it is not at all necessary that the "times" thus defined in different inertial systems agree with one another. One would have noticed this long ago if, for the practical experience of everyday life, light did not present (because of the large value of c) the means for fixing an absolute simultaneity.

The presuppositions of the existence (in principle) of (ideal, or perfect) measuring rods and clocks are not independent of each other; a light signal that is reflected back and forth between the ends of a rigid rod constitutes an ideal clock, provided that the postulate of the constancy of the light velocity in vacuum does not lead to contradictions.

The above paradox may then be formulated as follows. According to the rules of connection, used in classical physics, between the spatial coordinates and the time of events in the transition from one inertial system to another, the two assumptions of

(1) the constancy of the light velocity
(2) the independence of the laws (thus especially also of the law of the constancy of the light velocity) from the choice of inertial system (principle of special relativity)

are mutually incompatible (despite the fact that both taken separately are based on experience).

The insight fundamental for the special theory of relativity is this: The assumptions (1) and (2) are compatible if relations of a new type ("Lorentz transformation") are postulated for the conversion of coordinates and times of events. With the given physical interpretation of coordinates and time, this is by no means merely a conventional step but implies certain hypotheses concerning the actual behavior of moving measuring rods and clocks, which can be experimentally confirmed or disproved.

The universal principle of the special theory of relativity is contained in the postulate: The laws of physics are invariant with respect to Lorentz transformations (for the transition from one inertial system to any other arbitrarily chosen inertial system). This is a re-

ein einschränkendes Prinzip für die Naturgesetze, vergleichbar mit dem der Thermodynamik zugrunde liegenden einschränkenden Prinzip von der Nichtexistenz des *perpetuum mobile*.

Zunächst eine Bemerkung über die Beziehung der Theorie zum •vierdimensionalen Raum.• Es ist ein verbreiteter Irrtum, dass die spezielle Rel. Th. gewissermassen die Vierdimensionalität des physikalischen Kontinuums entdeckt bezw. neu eingeführt hätte. Dies ist natürlich nicht der Fall. Auch der klassischen Mechanik liegt das vierdimensionale Kontinuum von Raum und Zeit zugrunde. Nur haben im vierdimensionalen Kontinuum der klassischen Physik die •Schnitte• konstanten Zeitwertes eine absolute, d.h. von der Wahl des Bezugssystems unabhängige, Realität. Das vierdimensionale Kontinuum zerfällt dadurch natürlich in ein dreidimensionales und ein eindimensionales (Zeit), sodass die vierdimensionale Betrachtungsweise sich nicht als *notwendig* aufdrängt. Die spezielle Relativitätstheorie dagegen schafft eine formale Abhängigkeit zwischen der Art und Weise, wie die räumlichen Koordinaten einerseits und die Zeitkoordinate andrerseits in die Naturgesetze eingehen müssen.

Minkowskis wichtiger Beitrag zu der Theorie liegt in Folgendem: Vor Minkowskis Untersuchung hatte man an einem Gesetz eine Lorentz-Transformation auszuführen, um seine Invarianz bezüglich solcher Transformationen zu prüfen; ihm dagegen gelang es, einen solchen Formalismus einzuführen, dass die mathematische Form des Gesetzes selbst dessen Invarianz bezüglich Lorentz-Transformationen verbürgt. Er leistete durch Schaffung eines vierdimensionalen Tensorkalküls für den vierdimensionalen Raum dasselbe, was die gewöhnliche Vektorkalkül für die drei räumlichen Dimensionen leistet. Er zeigte auch, dass die Lorentz-Transformation (abgesehen von einem durch den besonderen Charakter der Zeit bedingten abweichenden Vorzeichen) nichts anderes ist als eine Drehung des Koordinatensystems im vierdimensionalen Raume.

Zunächst eine kritische Bemerkung zur Theorie, wie sie oben charakterisiert ist. Es fällt auf, dass die Theorie (ausser dem vierdimensionalen Raum) zweierlei physikalische Dinge einführt, nämlich (1) Massstäbe und Uhren, (2) alle sonstigen Dinge, z.B. das elektromagnetische Feld, den materiellen Punkt, usw. Dies ist in gewissem Sinne inkonsequent; Massstäbe und Uhren müssten eigent-

stricting principle for natural laws, comparable to the restricting principle of the nonexistence of the *perpetuum mobile* that underlies thermodynamics.

First a remark concerning the relation of the theory to "four-dimensional space." It is a widespread error that the special theory of relativity is supposed to have, to a certain extent, first discovered or, at any rate, newly introduced, the four-dimensionality of the physical continuum. This, of course, is not the case. Classical mechanics, too, is based on the four-dimensional continuum of space and time. But in the four-dimensional continuum of classical physics the subspaces with constant time value have an absolute reality, independent of the choice of the frame of reference. Because of this, the four-dimensional continuum breaks down naturally into a three-dimensional and a one-dimensional (time), so that the four-dimensional point of view does not force itself upon one as *necessary*. The special theory of relativity, on the other hand, creates a formal dependence between the way in which the space coordinates on the one hand, and the time coordinates on the other, must enter into the natural laws.

Minkowski's important contribution to the theory lies in the following: Before Minkowski's investigation it was necessary to carry out a Lorentz transformation on a law in order to test its invariance under such transformations; but he succeeded in introducing a formalism so that the mathematical form of the law itself guarantees its invariance under Lorentz transformations. By creating a four-dimensional tensor calculus, he achieved the same thing for the four-dimensional space that the ordinary vector calculus achieves for the three spatial dimensions. He also showed that the Lorentz transformation (apart from a different algebraic sign due to the special character of time) is nothing but a rotation of the coordinate system in the four-dimensional space.

First, a critical remark concerning the theory as it is characterized above. It is striking that the theory (except for the four-dimensional space) introduces two kinds of physical things, i.e., (1) measuring rods and clocks, (2) all other things, e.g., the electromagnetic field, the material point, etc. This, in a certain sense, is inconsistent; strictly speaking, measuring rods and clocks should emerge as solutions of

55

lich als Lösungen der Grundgleichungen (Gegenstände bestehend aus bewegten atomistischen Gebilden) dargestellt werden, nicht als gewissermassen theoretisch selbstständige Wesen. Das Vorgehen rechtfertigt sich aber dadurch, dass von Anfang an klar war, dass die Postulate der Theorie nicht stark genug sind, um aus ihr genügend vollständige Gleichungen für das physikalische Geschehen genügend frei von Willkür zu deduzieren, um auf eine solche Grundlage eine Theorie der Massstäbe und Uhren zu gründen. Wollte man nicht auf eine physikalische Deutung der Koordinaten überhaupt verzichten (was an sich möglich wäre), so war es besser, solche Inkonsequenz zuzulassen–allerdings mit der Verpflichtung, sie in einem späteren Stadium der Theorie zu eliminieren. Man darf aber die erwähnte Sünde nicht so weit legitimieren, dass man sich etwa vorstellt, dass Abstände physikalische Wesen besonderer Art seien, wesensverschieden von sonstigen physikalischen Grössen (-Physik auf Geometrie zurückführen,- usw.). Wir fragen nun nach den Erkenntnissen von definitivem Charakter, den die Physik der speziellen Relativitätstheorie verdankt.

(1) Es gibt keine Gleichzeitigkeit distanter Ereignisse; es gibt also auch keine unvermittelte Fernwirkung im Sinne der Newton'schen Mechanik. Die Einführung von Fernwirkungen, die sich mit Lichtgeschwindigkeit ausbreiten, bleibt zwar nach dieser Theorie denkbar, erscheint aber unnatürlich; in einer derartigen Theorie könnte es nämlich keinen vernünftigen Ausdruck für das Energieprinzip geben. Es erscheint deshalb unvermeidlich, dass die physikalische Realität durch kontinuierliche Raumfunktionen zu beschreiben ist. Der materielle Punkt dürfte deshalb als Grundbergriff der Theorie nicht mehr in Betracht kommen.

(2) Die Sätze der Erhaltung des Impulses und der Erhaltung der Energie werden zu einem einzigen Satz verschmolzen. Die träge Masse eines abgeschlossenen Systems ist mit seiner Energie identisch, sodass die Masse als selbstständiger Begriff eliminiert ist.

Bemerkung. Die Lichtgeschwindigkeit c ist eine der Grössen, welche in physikalischen Gleichungen als -universelle Konstante- auftritt. Wenn man aber als Zeiteinheit statt der Sekunde die Zeit einführt, in welcher das Licht 1 cm zurücklegt, so tritt c in den

the basic equations (objects consisting of moving atomic configurations), not, as it were, as theoretically self-sufficient entities. The procedure justifies itself, however, because it was clear from the very beginning that the postulates of the theory are not strong enough to deduce from them equations for physical events sufficiently complete and sufficiently free from arbitrariness in order to base upon such a foundation a theory of measuring rods and clocks. If one did not wish to forego a physical interpretation of the coordinates in general (something that, in itself, would be possible), it was better to permit such inconsistency–with the obligation, however, of eliminating it at a later stage of the theory. But one must not legitimize the sin just described so as to imagine that distances are physical entities of a special type, intrinsically different from other physical variables ("reducing physics to geometry," etc.).

We now shall inquire into the insights of a definitive nature that physics owes to the special theory of relativity.

(1) There is no such thing as simultaneity of distant events; consequently, there is also no such thing as immediate action at a distance in the sense of Newtonian mechanics. Although the introduction of actions at a distance, which propagate at the speed of light, remains feasible according to this theory, it appears unnatural; for in such a theory there could be no reasonable expression for the principle of conservation of energy. It therefore appears unavoidable that physical reality must be described in terms of continuous functions in space. The material point, therefore, can hardly be retained as a basic concept of the theory.

(2) The principles of the conservation of linear momentum and of energy are fused into one single principle. The inert mass of an isolated system is identical with its energy, thus eliminating mass as an independent concept.

Remark. The speed of light c is one of the quantities that occurs in physical equations as a "universal constant." If, however, one introduces as the unit of time, instead of the second, the time in which light travels 1 cm, c no longer occurs in the equations. In this sense

Gleichungen nicht mehr auf. Man kann in diesem Sinne sagen, dass die Konstante c nur eine *scheinbare* universelle Konstante ist.

Es ist offenkundig und allgemein angenommen, dass man auch noch zwei andere universelle Konstante dadurch aus der Physik eliminieren könnte, dass man an Stelle des Gramms und Centimeters passend gewählte »natürliche« Einheiten einführt (z.B. Masse und Radius des Elektrons).

Denkt man sich dies ausgeführt, so würden in den Grund-Gleichungen der Physik nur mehr »dimensionslose« Konstante auftreten können. Bezüglich dieser möchte ich einen Satz aussprechen, der vorläufig auf nichts anderes gegründet werden kann als auf ein Vertrauen in die Einfachheit, bezw. Verständlichkeit, der Natur; derartige *willkürliche* Konstante gibt es nicht; d.h. die Natur ist so beschaffen, dass man für sie logisch derart stark determinierte Gesetze aufstellen kann, dass in diesen Gesetzen nur rational völlig bestimmte Konstante auftreten (also nicht Konstante, deren Zahlwerte verändert werden könnten, ohne die Theorie zu zerstören).

Die spezielle Relativitätstheorie verdankt ihre Entstehung den Maxwell'schen Gleichungen des elektromagnetischen Feldes. Umgekehrt werden die letzteren erst durch die spezielle Relativitätstheorie in befriedigender Weise formal begriffen. Es sind die einfachsten Lorentz-invarianten Feldgleichungen, die für einen aus einem Vektorfeld abgeleiteten schief symmetrischen Tensor aufgestellt werden können. Dies wäre an sich befriedigend, wenn wir nicht aus den Quanten-Erscheinungen wüssten, dass die Maxwell'sche Theorie den energetischen Eigenschaften der Strahlung nicht gerecht wird. Wie aber die Maxwell'sche Theorie in natürlicher Weise modifiziert werden könnte, dafür liefert auch die spezielle Relativitätstheorie keinen hinreichenden Anhaltspunkt. Auch auf die Mach'sche Frage: »wie kommt es, dass die Inertialsysteme gegenüber anderen Koordinationssystemen physikalisch ausgezeichnet sind?« liefert diese Theorie keine Antwort.

Dass die spezielle Relativitätstheorie nur der erste Schritt einer notwendigen Entwicklung sei, wurde mir erst bei der Bemühung völlig klar die Gravitation im Rahmen dieser Theorie darzustellen. In der feldartig interpretierten klassischen Mechanik erscheint das

one could say that the constant *c* is only an *apparent* universal constant.

It is obvious and generally accepted that one could eliminate two more universal constants from physics by introducing, instead of the gram and the centimeter, properly chosen "natural" units (for example, mass and radius of the electron).

If one considers this done, then only "dimensionless" constants could occur in the basic equations of physics. Concerning such, I would like to state a proposition that at present cannot be based upon anything more than upon a faith in the simplicity, i.e., intelligibility, of nature: there are no *arbitrary* constants of this kind; that is to say, nature is so constituted that it is possible logically to lay down such strongly determined laws that within these laws only rationally completely determined constants occur (not constants, therefore, whose numerical value could be changed without destroying the theory).

The special theory of relativity owes its origin to Maxwell's equations of the electromagnetic field. Conversely, the latter can be grasped formally in satisfactory fashion only by way of the special theory of relativity. Maxwell's equations are the simplest Lorentz-invariant field equations that can be postulated for an antisymmetric tensor derived from a vector field. This in itself would be satisfactory, if we did not know from quantum phenomena that Maxwell's theory does not do justice to the energetic properties of radiation. But as to how Maxwell's theory would have to be modified in a natural fashion, for this even the special theory of relativity offers no adequate foothold. Also, to Mach's question: "how does it come about that inertial systems are physically distinguished above all other coordinate systems?" this theory offers no answer.

That the special theory of relativity is only the first step of a necessary development became completely clear to me only in my efforts to represent gravitation in the framework of this theory. In classical mechanics, interpreted in terms of the field, the potential

Potential der Gravitation als ein *skalares* Feld (die einfachste theoretische Möglichkeit eines Feldes mit einer einzigen Komponente). Eine solche Skalar-Theorie des Gravitationsfeldes kann zunächst leicht invariant gemacht werden inbezug auf die Gruppe der Lorentz-Transformationen. Folgendes Programm erscheint also natürlich: Das physikalische Gesamtfeld besteht aus einem Skalarfeld (Gravitation) und einem Vektorfeld (elektromagnetisches Feld); spätere Erkenntnisse mögen eventuell die Einführung noch komplizierterer Feldarten nötig machen, aber darum brauchte man sich zunächst nicht zu kümmern.

Die Möglichkeit der Realisierung dieses Programms war aber von vornherein zweifelhaft, weil die Theorie folgende Dinge vereinigen musste.

(1) Aus allgemeinen Überlegungen der speziellen Relativitätstheorie war klar, dass die *träge* Masse eines physikalischen Systems mit der Gesamtenergie (also z.B. mit der kinetischen Energie) wachse.

(2) Aus sehr präzisen Versuchen (insbesondere aus den Eötvös'schen Drehwage-Versuchen) war mit sehr grosser Präzision empirisch bekannt, dass die *schwere* Masse eines Körpers seiner *trägen* Masse genau gleich sei.

Aus (1) und (2) folgte, dass die *Schwere* eines Systems in genau bekannter Weise von seiner Gesamtenergie abhänge. Wenn die Theorie dies nicht oder nicht in natürlicher Weise leistete, so war sie zu verwerfen. Die Bedingung lässt sich am natürlichsten so aussprechen: die Fall-Beschleunigung eines Systems in einem gegebenen Schwerefelde ist von der Natur des fallenden Systems (speziell also auch von seinem Energie-Inhalte) unabhängig.

Es zeigte sich nun, dass im Rahmen des skizzierten Programmes diesem elementaren Sachverhalte überhaupt nicht oder jedenfalls nicht in natürlicher Weise Genüge geleistet werden konnte. Dies gab mir die Überzeugung, dass im Rahmen der speziellen Relativitätstheorie kein Platz sei für eine befriedigende Theorie der Gravitation.

Nun fiel mir ein: Die Tatsache der Gleichheit der trägen und schweren Masse, bezw. die Tatsache der Unabhängigkeit der Fallbeschleunigung von der Natur der fallenden Substanz, lässt sich so

of gravitation appears as a *scalar* field (the simplest theoretical possibility of a field with a single component). Such a scalar theory of the gravitational field can easily be made invariant under the group of Lorentz transformations. The following program appears natural, therefore: The total physical field consists of a scalar field (gravitation) and a vector field (electromagnetic field); later insights may eventually make necessary the introduction of still more complicated types of fields; but to begin with one did not need to bother about this.

The possibility of realization of this program was, however, in doubt from the very first, because the theory had to combine the following things:

(1) From the general considerations of special relativity theory it was clear that the inertial mass of a physical system increases with the total energy (therefore, e.g., with the kinetic energy).

(2) From very accurate experiments (especially from the torsion balance experiments of Eötvös) it was empirically known with very high accuracy that the gravitational mass of a body is exactly equal to its inertial mass.

It followed from (1) and (2) that the *weight* of a system depends in a precisely known manner on its total energy. If the theory did not accomplish this or could not do it naturally, it was to be rejected. The condition is most naturally expressed as follows: The acceleration of a system falling freely in a given gravitational field is independent of the nature of the falling system (especially therefore also of its energy content).

It turned out that, within the framework of the program sketched, this simple state of affairs could not at all, or at any rate not in any natural fashion, be represented in a satisfactory way. This convinced me that within the structure of the special theory of relativity there is no niche for a satisfactory theory of gravitation.

Now it came to me: the fact of the equality of inertial and gravitational mass, i.e., the fact of the independence of the gravitational acceleration from the nature of the falling substance, may be ex-

61

ausdrücken: In einem Gravitationsfelde (geringer räumlicher Ausdehnung) verhalten sich die Dinge so wie in einem gravitationsfreien Raume, wenn man in diesem statt eines ·Inertialsystems· ein gegen ein solches beschleunigtes Bezugssystem einführt.

Wenn man also das Verhalten der Körper inbezug auf das letztere Bezugssystem als durch ein ·wirkliches· (nicht nur scheinbares) Gravitationsfeld bedingt auffasst, so kann man dieses Bezugssystem mit dem gleichen Rechte als ein ·Inertialsystem· betrachten wie das ursprüngliche Bezugssystem.

Wenn man also beliebig ausgedehnte, nicht von vornherein durch räumliche Grenzbedingungen eingeschränkte, Gravitationsfelder als möglich betrachtet, so wird der Begriff des Inertialsystems völlig leer. Der Begriff ·Beschleunigung gegenüber dem Raume· verliert dann jede Bedeutung und damit auch das Trägheitsprinzip samt dem Mach'schen Paradoxon.

So führt die Tatsache der Gleichleit der trägen und schweren Masse ganz natürlich zu den Auffassungen, dass die Grund-Forderung der speziellen Relativitätstheorie (Invarianz der Gesetze bezüglich Lorentz-Transformationen) zu eng sei, d.h. dass man eine Invarianz der Gestze auch bezüglich *nicht linearer* Transformationen der Koordinaten im vierdimensionalen Kontinuum zu postulieren habe.

Dies trug sich 1908 zu. Warum brauchte es weiterer sieben Jahre für die Aufstellung der allgemeinen Rel. Theorie? Der hauptsächliche Grund liegt darin, dass man sich nicht so leicht von der Auffassung befreit, dass den Koordinaten eine unmittelbare metrische Bedeutung zukommen müsse. Die Wandlung vollzog sich ungefähr in folgender Weise.

Wir gehen aus von einem leeren, feldfreien Raume, wie er–auf ein Inertialsystem bezogen–im Sinne der speziellen Relativitätstheorie als der einfachste aller denkbaren physikalischen Tatbestände auftritt. Denken wir uns nun ein Nicht-Inertialsystem dadurch eingeführt, dass das neue System gegen das Inertialsystem (in dreidimensionaler Beschreibungsart) in einer Richtung (geeignet definiert) gleichförmig beschleunigt ist, so besteht inbezug auf dieses System ein statisches paralleles Schwerefeld. Das Bezugssystem kann dabei als starr gewählt werden, in den dreidimensionalen metrischen Beziehungen von euklidischem Charakter. Aber jene Zeit, in welcher

pressed as follows: In a gravitational field (of small spatial extension) things behave as they do in a space free of gravitation, if one introduces into it, in place of an "inertial system," a frame of reference accelerated relative to the former.

If then one interprets the behavior of a body with respect to the latter frame of reference as caused by a "real" (not merely apparent) gravitational field, it is possible to regard this frame as an "inertial system" with as much justification as the original reference system.

So, if one considers pervasive gravitational fields, not *a priori* restricted by spatial boundary conditions, physically possible, then the concept of "inertial system" becomes completely empty. The concept of "acceleration relative to space" then loses all meaning and with it the principle of inertia along with the paradox of Mach.

The fact of the equality of inertial and gravitational mass thus leads quite naturally to the recognition that the basic postulate of the special theory of relativity (invariance of the laws under Lorentz transformations) is too narrow, i.e., that an invariance of the laws must be postulated also relative to *nonlinear* transformations of the coordinates in the four-dimensional continuum.

This happened in 1908. Why were another seven years required for the construction of the general theory of relativity? The main reason lies in the fact that it is not so easy to free oneself from the idea that coordinates must have a direct metric significance. The transformation took place in approximately the following fashion.

We start with an empty, field-free space, as it occurs – related to an inertial system – within the meaning of the special theory of relativity, as the simplest of all imaginable physical situations. If we now think of a noninertial system introduced by assuming that the new system is uniformly accelerated against the inertial system (in a three-dimensional description) in one direction (conveniently defined), then there exists with reference to this system a static parallel gravitational field. The reference system may be chosen to be rigid, Euclidean in its three-dimensional metric properties. But the time in

das Feld statisch erscheint, wird *nicht* durch *gleich beschaffene* ruhende Uhren gemessen. Aus diesem speziellen Beispiel erkennt man schon, dass die unmittelbare metrische Bedeutung der Koordinaten verloren geht, wenn man überhaupt nichtlineare Transformationen der Koordinaten zulässt. Letzteres *muss* man aber, wenn man der Gleichheit von schwerer und träger Masse durch das Fundament der Theorie gerecht werden will, und wenn man das Mach'sche Paradoxon bezüglich der Inertialsysteme überwinden will.

Wenn man nun aber darauf verzichten muss, den Koordinaten eine unmittelbare metrische Bedeutung zu geben (Koordinatendifferenzen = messbare Längen bezw. Zeiten), so wird man nicht umhin können, alle durch kontinuierliche Transformationen der Koordinaten erzeugbare Koordinatensysteme als gleichwertig zu behandeln.

Die allgemeine Relativitätstheorie geht demgemäss von dem Grundsatz aus: Die Naturgesetze sind durch Gleichungen auszudrücken, die kovariant sind bezüglich der Gruppe der kontinuierlichen Koordinaten-Transformationen. Diese Gruppe tritt also hier an die Stelle der Gruppe der Lorentz-Transformationen der speziellen Relativitätstheorie, welch letztere Gruppe eine Untergruppe der ersteren bildet.

Diese Forderung für sich alleine genügt natürlich nicht als Ausgangspunkt für eine Ableitung der Grundgleichungen der Physik. Zunächst kann man sogar bestreiten, dass die Forderung allein eine wirkliche Beschränkung für die physikalischen Gesetze enthalte; denn es wird stets möglich sein, ein zunächst nur für gewisse Koordinatensysteme postuliertes Gesetz so umzuformulieren, dass die neue Formulierung der Form nach allgemein kovariant wird. Ausserdem ist es von vornherein klar, dass sich unendlich viele Feldgesetze formulieren lassen, die diese Kovarianz-Eigenschaft haben. Die eminente heuristische Bedeutung des allgemeinen Relativitätsprinzips liegt aber darin, dass es uns zu der Aufsuchung jener Gleichungssysteme führt, welche *in allgemein kovarianter* Formulierung *möglichst einfach* sind; unter diesen haben wir die Feldgesetze des physikalischen Raumes zu suchen. Felder, die durch solche Transformationen ineinander übergeführt werden können, beschreiben denselben realen Sachverhalt.

which the field appears as static is *not* measured by *equally constituted* stationary clocks. From this special example one can already recognize that the immediate metric significance of the coordinates is lost once one admits nonlinear transformations of the coordinates. To do the latter is, however, *obligatory* if one wants to do justice to the equality of gravitational and inertial mass through the foundations of the theory, and if one wants to overcome Mach's paradox regarding the inertial systems.

If, then, one must give up the notion of assigning to the coordinates an immediate metric meaning (differences of coordinates = measurable lengths, or times), one cannot but treat as equivalent all coordinate systems that can be created by the continuous transformations of the coordinates.

The general theory of relativity, accordingly, proceeds from the following principle: Natural laws are to be expressed by equations that are covariant under the group of continuous coordinate transformations. This group replaces the group of the Lorentz transformations of the special theory of relativity, which forms a subgroup of the former.

This postulate by itself is of course not sufficient to serve as point of departure for the derivation of the basic equations of physics. One might even deny, to begin with, that the postulate by itself involves a real restriction for the physical laws; for it will always be possible to reformulate a law, conjectured at first only for certain coordinate systems, so that the new formulation becomes formally generally covariant. Further, it is evident right away that an infinitely large number of field laws can be formulated that have this property of covariance. The eminent heuristic significance of the general principle of relativity is that it leads us to the search for those systems of equations that are *in their general covariant* formulation the *simplest ones possible*; among these we shall have to look for the field equations of physical space. Fields that can be transformed into each other by such transformations describe the same real situation.

Die Hauptfrage für den auf diesem Gebiete Suchenden ist diese: Von welcher mathematischen Art sind die Grössen (Funktionen der Koordinaten), welche die physikalischen Eigenschaften das Raumes auszudrücken gestatten (-Struktur-)? Dann erst: welchen Gleichungen genügen jene Grössen?

Wir können heute diese Fragen noch keineswegs mit Sicherheit beantworten. Der bei der ersten Formulierung der allgemeinen Rel. Theorie eingeschlagene Weg lässt sich so kennzeichnen. Wenn wir auch nicht wissen, durch was für Feldvariable (Struktur) der physikalische Raum zu charakterisieren ist, so kennen wir doch mit Sicherheit einen speziellen Fall: den des -feldfreien- Raumes in der speziellen Relativitätstheorie. Ein solcher Raum ist dadurch charakterisiert, dass für ein passend gewähltes Koordinatensystem der zu zwei benachbarten Punkten gehörige Ausdruck.

$$ds^2 = dx_1{}^2 + dx_2{}^2 - dx_3{}^2 - dx_4{}^2 \qquad (1)$$

eine messbare Grösse darstellt (Abstandsquadrat), also eine reale physikalische Bedeutung hat. Auf ein beliebiges System bezogen drückt sich diese Grösse so aus

$$ds^2 = g_{ik}dx_i dx_k \qquad (2)$$

wobei die Indices von 1 bis 4 laufen. Die g_{ik} bilden einen symmetrischen Tensor. Wenn, nach Ausführung einer Transformation am Felde (1), die ersten Ableitungen der g_{ik} nach den Koordinaten nicht verschwinden, so besteht, mit Bezug auf dies Koordinatensystem, ein Gravitationsfeld im Sinne der obigen Überlegung, und zwar ein Gravitationsfeld ganz spezieller Art. Dies besondere Feld lässt sich dank der Riemann'schen Untersuchung n-dimensionaler metrischer Räume invariant charakterisieren:

(1) Der aus den Koeffizienten der Metrik (2) gebildete Riemann'sche Krümmungstensor R_{iklm} verschwindet.

(2) Die Bahn eines Massenpunktes ist inbezug auf das Inertialsystem (inbezug auf welches (1) gilt) eine gerade Linie, also eine Extremale (Geodete). Letzteres ist aber bereits eine auf (2) sich stützende Charakterisierung des Bewegungsgesetzes.

66

The major question for anyone searching in this field is this: Of which mathematical type are the variables (functions of the co-ordinates) that permit the expression of the physical properties of space ("structure")? Only after that: Which equations are satisfied by those variables?

The answer to these questions is today by no means certain. The path chosen by the first formulation of the general theory of relativity can be characterized as follows. Even though we do not know by what kind of field variables (structure) physical space is to be characterized, we do know with certainty a special case: that of the "field-free" space in the special theory of relativity. Such a space is characterized by the fact that for a properly chosen coordinate system the expression

$$ds^2 = dx_1^2 + dx_2^2 + dx_3^2 - dx_4^2 \qquad (1)$$

belonging to two neighboring points, represents a measurable quantity (square of distance), and thus has a real physical meaning. Referred to an arbitrary system this quantity is expressed as follows:

$$ds^2 = g_{ik}dx_i dx_k \qquad (2)$$

whereby the indices run from 1 to 4. The g_{ik} form a (real) symmetrical tensor. If, after carrying out a transformation on field (1), the first derivatives of the g_{ik} with respect to the coordinates do not vanish, there exists a gravitational field with reference to this system of coordinates in the sense of the above consideration, but of a very special type. Thanks to Riemann's investigation of n-dimensional metric spaces, this special field can be characterized invariantly:

(1) Riemann's curvature-tensor R_{iklm}, formed from the coefficients of the metric (2), vanishes.
(2) The trajectory of a mass-point in reference to the inertial system (relative to which (1) is valid) is a straight line, hence an extremal (geodesic). This last statement, however, is already a characterization of the law of motion based on (2).

Das *allgemeine* Gesetz des physikalischen Raumes muss nun eine Verallgemeinerung des soeben charakterisierten Gesetzes sein. Ich nahm nun an, dass es zwei Stufen der Verallgemeinerung gibt:

(a) reines Gravitationsfeld
(b) allgemeines Feld (in welchem auch Grössen auftreten, die irgendwie dem elektromagnetischen Felde entsprechen).

Der Fall (a) war dadurch charakterisiert, dass das Feld zwar immer noch durch eine Riemann-Metrik (2) bezw. durch einen symmetrischen Tensor darstellbar ist, wobei es aber (ausser im Infinitesimalen) keine Darstellung in der Form (1) gibt. Dies bedeutet, dass im Falle (a) der Riemann-Tensor *nicht* verschwindet. Es ist aber klar, dass in diesem Falle ein Feldgesetz gelten muss, das eine Verallgemeinerung (Abschwächung) dieses Gesetzes ist. Soll auch dies Gesetz von der zweiten Differentiationsordnung und in den zweiten Ableitungen linear sein, so kam nur die durch einmalige Kontraktion zu gewinnende Gleichung

$$0 = R_{kl} = g^{im} R_{iklm}$$

als Feldgleichung im Falle (a) in Betracht. Es erscheint ferner natürlich anzunehmen, dass auch im Falle (a) die geodätische Linie immer noch das Bewegungsgesetz des materiellen Punktes darstelle.

Es erschien mir damals aussichtslos, den Versuch zu wagen, das Gesamtfeld (b) darzustellen und für dieses Feldgesetze zu ermitteln. Ich zog es deshalb vor, einen vorläufigen formalen Rahmen für eine Darstellung der ganzen physikalischen Realität hinzustellen; dies war nötig, um wenigstens vorläufig die Brauchbarkeit des Grundgedankens der allgemeinen Relativität untersuchen zu können. Dies geschah so.

In der Newton'schen Theorie kann man als Feldgesetz der Gravitation

$$\Delta \phi = 0$$

schreiben (ϕ = Gravitationspotential) an solchen Orten, wo die Dichte ρ der Materie verschwindet. Allgemein wäre zu setzen (Poissonsche Gleichung)

$$\Delta \phi = 4 \pi k \rho \quad (\rho = \text{Massen-Dichte}).$$

The *universal* law of physical space must be a generalization of the law just characterized. I now assumed that there are two steps of generalization:

(a) the pure gravitational field
(b) the general field (which is also to include quantities that somehow correspond to the electromagnetic field).

The case (a) was characterized by the fact that the field can still be represented by a Riemann metric (2), i.e., by a symmetric tensor, but without a representation of the form (1) (save on an infinitesimal scale). This means that in the case (a) the Riemann tensor does not vanish. It is clear, however, that in this case a field law must hold that is some generalization (loosening) of this law. If this generalized law also is to be of the second order of differentiation and linear in the second derivatives, then only the equation obtained by a single contraction

$$0 = R_{kl} = g^{im}R_{iklm}$$

was a prospective field law in the case (a). It appears natural, moreover, to assume that also in the case (a) the geodesic line is still to represent the law of motion of the material point.

It seemed hopeless to me at that time to venture the attempt of representing the total field (b) and to ascertain field laws for it. I preferred, therefore, to set up a preliminary formal frame for the representation of the entire physical reality; this was necessary in order to be able to investigate, at least preliminarily, the effectiveness of the basic idea of general relativity. This was done as follows.

In Newton's theory one can write the field law of gravitation thus:

$$\nabla^2\phi = 0$$

(ϕ = gravitation potential), valid wherever the density of matter, ρ, vanishes. In general one has (Poisson's equation)

$$\nabla^2\phi = 4\pi k\rho \ (\rho = \text{mass density}).$$

Im Falle der relativistischen Theorie des Gravitationsfeldes tritt R_{ik} an die Stelle von $\triangle\phi$. Auf die rechte Seite haben wir dann an die Stelle von ρ ebenfalls einen Tensor zu setzen. Da wir aus der speziellen Rel. Th. wissen, dass die (träge) Masse gleich ist der Energie, so wird auf die rechte Seite der Tensor der Energie-Dichte zu setzen sein – genauer der gesamten Energiedichte, soweit sie nicht dem reinen Gravitationsfelde angehört. Man gelangt so zu den Feldgleichungen

$$R_{ik} - \tfrac{1}{2}\,g_{ik}\,R = -k\,T_{ik}.$$

Das zweite Glied der linken Seite ist aus formalen Gründen zugefügt; die linke Seite ist nämlich so geschrieben, dass ihre Divergenz im Sinne des absoluten Differentialkalküls identisch verschwindet. Die rechte Seite ist eine formale Zusammenfassung aller Dinge, deren Erfassung im Sinne einer Feldtheorie noch problematisch ist. Natürlich war ich keinen Augenblick darüber im Zweifel, dass diese Fassung nur ein Notbehelf war, um dem allgemeinen Relativitätsprinzip einen vorläufigen geschlossenen Ausdruck zu geben. Es war ja nicht wesentlich *mehr* als eine Theorie des Gravitationsfeldes, das einigermassen künstlich von einem Gesamtfelde noch unbekannter Struktur isoliert wurde.

Wenn irgend etwas – abgesehen von der Forderung der Invarianz der Gleichungen bezüglich der Gruppe der kontinuierlichen Koordinaten-Transformationen – in der skizzierten Theorie möglicherweise endgültige Bedeutung beanspruchen kann, so ist es die Theorie des Grenzfalles des reinen Gravitationsfeldes und dessen Beziehung zu der metrischen Struktur des Raumes. Deshalb soll im unmittelbar Folgenden nur von den Gleichungen des reinen Gravitationsfeldes die Rede sein.

Das Eigenartige an diesen Gleichungen ist einerseits ihr komplizierter Bau, besonders ihr nichtlinearer Charakter inbezug auf die Feldvariabeln und deren Ableitungen, andererseits, die fast zwingende Notwendigkeit, mit welcher die Transformationsgruppe dies komplizierte Feldgesetz bestimmt. Wenn man bei der speziellen Relativitätstheorie, d.h. bei der Invarianz bezüglich der Lorentz-Gruppe, stehen geblieben wäre, so würde auch im Rahmen dieser engeren Gruppe das Feldgesetz $R_{ik} = 0$ invariant sein. Aber vom Standpunkte

70

In the relativistic theory of the gravitational field, R_{ik} takes the place of $\nabla^2 \phi$. On the right-hand side we shall then have to replace ρ also by a tensor. Since we know from the special theory of relativity that the (inertial) mass equals the energy, we shall have to put on the right-hand side the tensor of energy density – more precisely, of the entire energy density that does not belong to the pure gravitational field. In this way one arrives at the field equation

$$R_{ik} - \tfrac{1}{2} g_{ik} R = -k T_{ik}.$$

The second member on the left-hand side is added because of formal considerations; for the left-hand side is written in such a way that its divergence, in the sense of the absolute differential calculus, vanishes identically. The right-hand side is a formal condensation of all things whose comprehension in the sense of a field theory is still problematic. Not for a moment, of course, did I doubt that this formulation was merely a makeshift in order to give the general principle of relativity a preliminary closed-form expression. For it was essentially *no more* than a theory of the gravitational field, which was isolated somewhat artificially from a total field of as yet unknown structure.

If anything in the theory as sketched – apart from the postulate of invariance of the equations under the group of continuous coordinate transformations – can possibly be claimed to be definitive, then it is the theory of the limiting case of a pure gravitational field and its relation to the metric structure of space. For this reason, in what immediately follows we shall speak only of the equations of the pure gravitational field.

The peculiarity of these equations lies, on the one hand, in their complicated structure, especially their nonlinear character with respect to the field variables and their derivatives, and, on the other hand, in the almost compelling necessity with which the transformation group determines this complicated field law. If one had stopped with the special theory of relativity, i.e., with the invariance under the Lorentz group, then the field law $R_{ik}=0$ would remain invariant also within the frame of this narrower group. But, from

der engeren Gruppe bestünde zunächst keinerlei Anlass dafür, dass die Gravitation durch eine so komplizierte Struktur dargestellt werden müsse, wie sie der symmetrische Tensor g_{ik} darstellt. Würde man aber doch hinreichende Gründe dafür finden, so gäbe es eine unübersehbare Zahl von Feldgesetzen aus Grössen g_{ik} die alle kovariant sind bezüglich Lorentz-Transformationen (nicht aber gegenüber der allgemeinen Gruppe). Selbst aber wenn man von all den denkbaren Lorentz-invarianten Gesetzen zufällig gerade das zu der weiteren Gruppe gehörige Gesetz erraten hätte, so wäre man immer noch nicht auf der durch das allgemeine Relativitätsprinzip erlangten Stufe der Erkenntnis. Denn vom Standpunkt der Lorentz-Gruppe wären zwei Lösungen fälschlich als physikalisch voneinander verschieden zu betrachten, wenn sie durch eine nichtlineare Koordinaten-Transformation ineinander transformierbar sind, d.h. vom Standpunkt der weiteren Gruppe nur verschiedene Darstellungen desselben Feldes sind.

Noch eine allgemeine Bemerkung über Struktur und Gruppe. Es ist klar, dass man im Allgemeinen eine Theorie als umso volkommener beurteilen wird, eine je einfacherer -Struktur- sie zugrundelegt und je weiter die Gruppe ist, bezüglich welcher die Feldgleichungen invariant sind. Man sieht nun, dass diese beiden Forderungen einander im Wege sind. Gemäss der speziellen Relativitätstheorie (Lorentz-Gruppe) kann man z.B. für die denkbar einfachste Struktur (skalares Feld) ein kovariantes Gesetz aufstellen, während es in der allgemeinen Relativitätstheorie (weitere Gruppe der kontinuierlichen Koordinaten-Transformationen) erst für die kompliziertere Struktur des symmetrischen Tensors ein invariantes Feldgesetz gibt. Wir haben *physikalische* Gründe dafür angegeben, dass Invarianz gegenüber der weiteren Gruppe in der Physik gefordert werden muss;[1] vom rein mathematischen Gesichtspunkte aus sehe ich keinen Zwang, die einfachere Struktur der Weite der Gruppe zum Opfer zu bringen.

Die Gruppe der allgemeinen Relativität bringt es zum ersten Male mit sich, dass das einfachste invariante Gesetz nicht linear und homogen in den Feldvariabeln und ihren Differentialquotienten ist. Dies ist

[1] Bei der engeren Gruppe zu bleiben und gleichzeitig die kompliziertere Struktur der allgemeinen Rel. Theorie zugrunde zu legen, bedeutet eine naive Inkonsequenz. Sünde bleibt Sünde, auch wenn sie von sonst respektabeln Männern begangen wird.

the point of view of the narrower group, there would be no off-hand grounds for representing gravitation by a structure as involved as the symmetric tensor g_{ik}. If, nonetheless, one would find sufficient reasons for it, there would then arise an immense number of field laws out of quantities g_{ik}, all of which are covariant under Lorentz transformations (not, however, under the general group). Even if, however, of all the conceivable Lorentz-invariant laws, one had accidentally guessed precisely the law belonging to the wider group, one would still not have achieved the level of understanding corresponding to the general principle of relativity. For, from the standpoint of the Lorentz group, two solutions would incorrectly have to be viewed as physically different if they can be transformed into each other by a nonlinear transformation of coordinates, i.e., if from the point of view of the wider group they are merely different representations of the same field.

One more general remark concerning structure and group. It is clear that in general one will judge a theory to be the more nearly perfect the simpler a "structure" it postulates and the broader the group concerning which the field equations are invariant. One sees now that these two desiderata get in each other's way. For example: according to the special theory of relativity (Lorentz group) one can set up a covariant law for the simplest structure imaginable (a scalar field), whereas in the general theory of relativity (wider group of the continuous transformations of coordinates) there is an invariant field law only for the more complicated structure of the symmetric tensor. We have already given *physical* reasons for the fact that in physics invariance under the wider group has to be required:[1] from a purely mathematical standpoint I can see no necessity for sacrificing the simpler structure to the generality of the group.

The group of general relativity is the first one requiring that the simplest invariant law be no longer linear and homogeneous in the field variables and their derivatives. This is of fundamental impor-

---

[1] To remain with the narrower group and at the same time to base the relativity theory of gravitation upon the more complicated [tensor-] structure implies a naive inconsequence. Sin remains sin, even if it is committed by otherwise ever so respectable men.

aus folgendem Grunde von fundamentaler Wichtigkeit. Ist das Feldgesetz linear (und homogen), so ist die Summe zweier Lösungen wieder eine Lösung; so ist es z.B. bei den Maxwell'schen Feldgleichungen des leeren Raumes. In einer solchen Theorie kann aus dem Feldgesetz allein nicht auf eine Wechselwirkung von Gebilden geschlossen werden, die isoliert durch Lösungen des Systems dargestellt werden können. Daher bedurfte es in den bisherigen Theorien neben den Feldgesetzen besonderer Gesetze für die Bewegung der materiellen Gebilde unter dem Einfluss der Felder. In der relativistischen Gravitationstheorie wurde nun zwar ursprünglich neben dem Feldgesetz das Bewegungsgesetz (Geodätische Linie) unabhängig postuliert. Es hat sich aber nachträglich herausgestellt, dass das Bewegungsgesetz nicht unabhängig angenommen werden muss (und darf), sondern dass es in dem Gesetz des Gravitationsfeldes implicite enthalten ist.

Das Wesen dieser an sich komplizierten Sachlage kann man sich wie folgt veranschaulichen. Ein einziger ruhender materieller Punkt wird durch ein Gravitationsfeld repräsentiert, das überall endlich und regulär ist ausser an dem Orte, an dem der materielle Punkt sitzt; dort hat das Feld eine Singularität. Berechnet man aber durch Integration der Feldgleichungen das Feld, welches zu zwei ruhenden materiellen Punkten gehört, so hat dieses ausser den Singularitäten am Orte der materiellen Punkte noch eine aus singulären Punkten bestehende Linie, welche die beiden Punkte verbindet. Man kann aber eine Bewegung der materiellen Punkte in solcher Weise vorgeben, dass das durch sie bestimmte Gravitationsfeld ausserhalb der materiellen Punkte nirgends singulär wird. Es sind dies gerade jene Bewegungen, die in erster Näherung durch die Newton'schen Gesetze beschrieben werden. Man kann also sagen: Die Massen bewegen sich so, dass die Feldgleichung im Raume ausserhalb der Massen nirgends Singularitäten des Feldes bedingt. Diese Eigenschaft der Gravitationsgleichungen hängt unmittelbar zusammen mit ihrer Nicht-Linearität, und diese ihrerseits wird durch die weitere Transformationsgruppe bedingt.

Nun könnte man allerdings den Einwand machen: Wenn am Orte der materiellen Punkte Singularitäten zugelassen werden, was für eine Berechtigung besteht dann, das Auftreten von Singularitäten

tance for the following reason. If the field law is linear (and homogeneous), then the sum of two solutions is again a solution; so it is, for example, in Maxwell's field equations for the vacuum. In such a theory it is impossible to deduce from the field equations alone an interaction between structures that separately represent solutions of the system. That is why all theories up to now required, in addition to the field equations, special equations for the motion of material bodies under the influence of the fields. In the relativistic theory of gravitation, it is true, the law of motion (geodesic line) was originally postulated independently in addition to the field law. Subsequently, though, it turned out that the law of motion need not (and must not) be assumed independently, but that it is already implicitly contained within the law of the gravitational field.

The essence of this truly involved situation can be visualized as follows: A single material point at rest will be represented by a gravitational field that is everywhere finite and regular, except where the material point is located: there the field has a singularity. If, however, one computes the field belonging to two material points at rest by integrating the field equations, then this field has in addition to the singularities at the positions of the material points a curve of singular points connecting the two points. It is possible, however, to stipulate a motion of the material points so that the gravitational field determined by them does not become singular anywhere except at the material points. These are precisely those motions described in first approximation by Newton's laws. One may say, therefore: The masses move in such fashion that the solution of the field equations is nowhere singular except at the mass points. This property of the gravitational equations is intimately connected with their nonlinearity, and this, in turn, results from the wider group of transformations.

Now it would of course be possible to object: If singularities are permitted at the locations of the material points, what justification is there for forbidding the occurrence of singularities else-

im übrigen Raume zu verbieten? Dieser Einwand wäre dann berechtigt, wenn die Gleichungen der Gravitation als Gleichungen des Gesamtfeldes anzusehen wären. So aber wird man sagen müssen, dass das Feld eines materiellen Teilchens desto weniger als *reines Gravitationsfeld* wird betrachtet werden dürfen, je näher man dem eigentlichen Ort des Teilchens kommt. Würde man die Feldgleichung des Gesamtfeldes haben, so müsste man verlangen, dass die Teilchen selbst als *überall* singularitätsfreie Lösungen der vollständigen Feldgleichungen sich darstellen lassen. Dann erst wäre die allgemeine Relativitätstheorie eine *vollständige* Theorie.

Bevor ich auf die Frage der Vollendung der allgemeinen Relativitätstheorie eingehe, muss ich Stellung nehmen zu der erfolgreichsten physikalischen Theorie unserer Zeit, der statistischen Quantentheorie, die vor etwa fünfundzwanzig Jahren eine konsistente logische Form angenommen hat (Schrödinger, Heisenberg, Dirac, Born). Es ist die einzige gegenwärtige Theorie, welche die Erfahrungen über den Quanten-Charakter der mikromechanischen Vorgänge einheitlich zu begreifen gestattet. Diese Theorie auf der einen Seite und die Relativitätstheorie auf der andern Seite werden beide in gewissem Sinne für richtig gehalten, obwohl ihre Verschmelzung allen bisherigen Bemühungen widerstanden hat. Damit hängt es wohl zusammen, dass unter den theoretischen Physikern der Gegenwart durchaus verschiedene Meinungen darüber bestehen, wie das theoretische Fundament der künftigen Physik aussehen wird. Ist es eine Feldtheorie; ist es eine im Wesentlichen statistische Theorie? Ich will hier kurz sagen, wie ich daüber denke.

Die Physik ist eine Bemühung das Seiende als etwas begrifflich zu erfassen, was unabhängig vom Wahrgenommen-Werden gedacht wird. In diesem Sinne spricht man vom »Physikalisch-Realen.« In der Vor-Quantenphysik war kein Zweifel, wie dies zu verstehen sei. In Newtons Theorie war das Reale durch materielle Punkte in Raum und Zeit, in der Maxwell'schen Theorie durch ein Feld in Raum und Zeit dargestellt. In der Quantenmechanik ist es weniger durchsichtig. Wenn man fragt: Stellt eine Ψ-Funktion der Quantentheorie einen realen Sachverhalt in demselben Sinne dar wie ein materielles Punktsystem oder ein elektromagnetisches Feld, so zögert man mit der simpeln Antwort »ja« oder »nein«; warum? Was die Ψ-Funktion

where? This objection would be justified if the equations of gravitation were to be considered as equations of the total field. [Since this is not the case], however, one will have to say that the field of a material particle will differ the more from a *pure gravitational field* the closer one comes to the location of the particle. If one had the field equations of the total field, one would be compelled to demand that the particles themselves could be represented as solutions of the complete field equations that are free of irregularities everywhere. Only then would the general theory of relativity be a *complete* theory.

Before I enter upon the question of the completion of the general theory of relativity, I must take a stand with reference to the most successful physical theory of our period, viz., the statistical quantum theory, which assumed a consistent logical form about twenty-five years ago, (Schrödinger, Heisenberg, Dirac, Born). At present this is the only theory that permits a unitary grasp of experiences concerning the quantum character of micro-mechanical events. This theory, on the one hand, and the theory of relativity on the other, are both considered correct in a certain sense, although all efforts to fuse them into a single whole so far have not met with success. This is probably why among contemporary theoretical physicists there exist entirely differing opinions as to what the theoretical foundation of the physics of the future will look like. Will it be a field theory? Will it be in essence a statistical theory? I shall briefly indicate my own thoughts on this point.

Physics is an attempt conceptually to grasp reality as something that is considered to be independent of its being observed. In this sense one speaks of "physical reality." In pre-quantum physics there was no doubt as to how this was to be understood. In Newton's theory reality was determined by a material point in space and time, in Maxwell's theory by the field in space and time. In quantum mechanics the situation is less transparent. If one asks: does a Ψ-function of the quantum theory represent a real fact in the same sense as a material system of points or an electromagnetic field? one hesitates to reply with a simple "yes" or "no." Why? What the Ψ-

(zu einer bestimmten Zeit) aussagt, das ist: Welches ist die Wahrscheinlichkeit dafür, eine bestimmte physikalische Grösse q (oder p) in einem bestimmten gegebenen Intervall vorzufinden, wenn ich sie zur Zeit t messe? Die Wahrscheinlichkeit ist hierbei als eine empirisch feststellbare, also gewiss »reale« Grösse anzusehen, die ich feststellen kann, wenn ich dieselbe Ψ-Funktion sehr oft erzeuge und jedesmal eine q-Messung vornehme. Wie steht es nun aber mit dem einzelnen gemessenen Wert von q? Hatte das betreffende individuelle System diesen q-Wert schon vor der Messung? Auf diese Frage gibt es im Rahmen der Theorie keine bestimmte Antwort, weil ja die Messung ein Prozess ist, der einen endlichen äusseren Eingriff in das System bedeutet; es wäre daher denkbar, dass das System einen bestimmten Zahlwert für q (bezw. p) den gemessenen Zahlwert erst durch die Messung selbt erhält. Für die weitere Diskussion denke ich mir zwei Physiker A und B, die bezüglich des durch die Ψ-Funktion beschriebenen realen Zustandes eine verschiedene Auffassung vertreten.

A. Das einzelne System hat (vor der Messung) einen bestimmten Wert von q (bezw. p) für alle Variabeln des Systems, und zwar *den* Wert, der bei einer Messung dieser Variabeln festgestellt wird. Ausgehend von dieser Auffassung wird er erklären: Die Ψ-Funktion ist keine erschöpfende Darstellung des realen Zustandes des Systems, sondern eine unvollständige Darstellung; sie drückt nur dasjenige aus, was wir auf Grund früherer Messungen über das System wissen.

B. Das einzelne System hat (vor der Messung) keinen bestimmten Wert von q (bezw. p). Der Messwert kommt unter Mitwirkung der ihm vermöge der Ψ-Funktion eigentümlichen Wahrscheinlichkeit erst durch den Akt der Messung zustande. Ausgehend von dieser Auffassung wird (oder wenigstens darf) er erklären: Die Ψ-Funktion ist eine erschöpfende Darstellung des realen Zustandes des Systems.

Nun präsentieren wir diesen beiden Physikern folgenden Fall. Es liege ein System vor das zu der Zeit t unserer Betrachtung aus zwei Teilsystemen S_1 und S_2 bestehe, die zu dieser Zeit räumlich getrennt

function (at a definite time) states, is this: What is the probability for finding a definite physical quantity q (or p) in a definite given interval if I measure it at time t? The probability is here to be viewed as an empirically determinable, and therefore certainly a "real" quantity, which I may determine if I create the same Ψ-function very often and each time perform a q-measurement. But what about the single measured value of q? Did the respective individual system have this q-value even before the measurement? To this question there is no definite answer within the framework of the [existing] theory, since the measurement is a process that implies a finite disturbance of the system from the outside; it would therefore be conceivable that the system obtains a definite numerical value for q (or p), the measured numerical value, only through the measurement itself. For the further discussion I shall assume two physicists, A and B, who represent different conceptions concerning the real situation as described by the Ψ-function.

A. The individual system (before the measurement) has a definite value of q (or p) for all variables of the system, specifically *that* value which is determined by a measurement of this variable. Proceeding from this conception, he will state: The Ψ-function is not a complete description of the exact state of the system, but only an incomplete representation; it expresses only what we know about the system because of previous measurements.

B. The individual system (before the measurement) has no definite value of q (or p). The measured value is produced by the act of measurement itself consistent with the probability appropriate to the Ψ-function. Proceeding from this conception, he will (or, at least, he may) state: The Ψ-function is an exhaustive description of the real situation of the system.

Now we present to these two physicists the following case. There is to be a system that at the time t of our observation consists of two component systems S_1 and S_2, which at this time are spatially separated and (in the sense of the classical physics) interact with

und (im Sinne der klassischen Physik) ohne erhebliche Wechselwir kung sind. Das Gesamtsystem sei durch eine bekannte Ψ-Funktior Ψ_{12} im Sinne der Quantenmechanik vollständig beschrieben. Alle Quantentheoretiker stimmen nun im Folgenden überein. Wenn ich eine vollständige Messung an S_1 mache, so erhalte ich aus den Mess resultaten und aus Ψ_{12} eine völlig bestimmte Ψ-Funktion Ψ_2 des Systems S_2. Der Charakter von Ψ_2 hängt dann davon ab, was *für eine Art* Messung ich an S_1 vornehme. Nun scheint es mir, dass man von dem realen Sachverhalt des Teilsystems S_2 sprechen kann. Von die sem realen Sachverhalt wissen wir vor der Messung and S_1 von vorn herein noch weniger als bei einem durch die Ψ-Funktion beschrie benen System. Aber an *einer* Annahme sollten wir nach meiner Ansicht unbedingt festhalten: Der reale Sachverhalt (Zustand) des Systems S_2 ist unabhängig davon, was mit dem von ihm räumlich getrennten System S_1 vorgenommen wird. Je nach der Art der Mes sung, welche ich an S_1 vornehme, bekomme ich aber ein andersar tiges Ψ_2 für das zweite Teilsystem. (Ψ_2, $\Psi_2{}^1 \ldots$). Nun muss aber der Realzustand von S_2 unabhängig davon sein, was an S_1 geschieht. Für denselben Realzustand von S_2 können also (je nach Wahl der Mes sung an S_1) verschiedenartige Ψ-Funktionen gefunden werden. (Die sem Schlusse kann man nur dadurch ausweichen, dass man ent weder annimmt, dass die Messung an S_1 den Realzustand von S_2 (telepathisch) verändert, oder aber dass man Dingen, die räumlich voneinander getrennt sind, unabhängige Realzustände überhaupt abspricht. Beides scheint mir ganz unakzeptabel.)

Wenn nun die Physiker A und B diese Überlegung als stich haltig annehmen, so wird B seinen Standpunkt aufgeben müssen, dass die Ψ-Funktion eine vollständige Beschreibung eines realen Sachverhaltes sei. Denn es wäre in diesem Falle unmöglich, dass demselben Sachverhalt (von S_2) zwei verschiedenartige Ψ-Funk tionen zugeordnet werden könnten.

Der statistische Charakter der gegenwärtigen Theorie würde dann eine notwendige Folge der Unvollständigkeit der Beschreibung der Systeme in der Quantenmechanik sein, und es bestände kein Grund mehr für die Annahme, dass eine zukünftige Basis der Physik auf Statistik gegründet sein müsse.

each other but slightly. The total system is to be described completely in terms of quantum mechanics by a known Ψ-function, say Ψ_{12}. All quantum theoreticians now agree upon the following. If I make a complete measurement of S_1, I obtain from the results of the measurement and from Ψ_{12} an entirely definite Ψ-function Ψ_2 of the system S_2. The character of Ψ_2 then depends upon *what kind* of measurement I perform on S_1.

Now it appears to me that one may speak of the real state of the partial system S_2. To begin with, before performing the measurement on S_1, we know even less of this real state than we know of a system described by the Ψ-function. But on one assumption we should, in my opinion, insist without qualification: the real state of the system S_2 is independent of any manipulation of the system S_1, which is spatially separated from the former. According to the type of measurement I perform on S_1, I get, however, a very different Ψ_2 for the second partial system (Ψ_2, $\Psi_2{}^1$, . . .). Now, however, the real state of S_2 must be independent of what happens to S_1. For the same real state of S_2 it is possible therefore to find (depending on one's choice of the measurement performed on S_1) different types of Ψ-function. (One can escape from this conclusion only by either assuming that the measurement of S_1 (telepathically) changes the real state of S_2 or by denying altogether that spatially separated entities possess independent real states. Both alternatives appear to me entirely unacceptable.)

If now the physicists A and B accept this reasoning as valid, then B will have to give up his position that the Ψ-function constitutes a complete description of a real state. For in this case it would be impossible that two different types of Ψ-functions could be assigned to the identical state of S_2.

The statistical character of the present theory would then follow necessarily from the incompleteness of the description of the systems in quantum mechanics, and there would no longer exist any ground for the assumption that a future foundation of physics must be based upon statistics.

Meine Meinung ist die, dass die gegenwärtige Quantentheorie bei gewissen festgelegten Grundbegriffen, die im Wesentlichen der klassischen Mechanik entnommen sind, eine optimale Formulierung der Zusammenhänge darstellt. Ich glaube aber, dass diese Theorie keinen brauchbaren Ausgangspunkt für die künftige Entwicklung bietet. Dies ist der Punkt, in welchem meine Erwartung von derjenigen der meisten zeitgenössischen Physiker abweicht. Sie sind davon überzeugt, dass den wesentlichen Zügen der Quantenphänomene (scheinbar sprunghafte und zeitlich nicht determinierte Änderungen des Zustandes eines Systems, gleichzeitig korpuskuläre und undulatorische Qualitäten der elementaren energetischen Gebilde) nicht Rechnung getragen werden kann durch eine Theorie, die den Realzustand der Dinge durch kontinuierliche Funktionen des Raumes beschreibt, für welche Differentialgleichungen gelten. Sie denken auch, dass man auf solchem Wege die atomistische Struktur der Materie und Strahlung nicht wird verstehen können. Sie erwarten, dass Systeme von Differentialgleichungen, wie sie für eine solche Theorie in Betracht kämen, überhaupt keine Lösungen haben, die überall im vierdimensionalen Raume regulär (singularitätsfrei) sind. Vor allem aber glauben sie, dass der anscheinend sprunghafte Charakter der Elementarvorgänge nur durch eine im Wesen statistische Theorie dargestellt werden kann, in welcher den sprunghaften Änderungen der Systeme durch *kontinuierliche* Änderungen von Wahrscheinlichkeiten der möglichen Zustände Rechnung getragen wird.

All diese Bemerkungen erscheinen mir recht eindrucksvoll. Die Frage, auf die es ankommt, scheint mir aber die zu sein: Was kann bei der heutigen Situation der Theorie mit einiger Aussicht auf Erfolg versucht werden? Da sind es die Erfahrungen in der Gravitationstheorie, die für meine Erwartungen richtung-gebend sind. Diese Gleichungen haben nach meiner Ansicht mehr Aussicht, etwas *Genaues* auszusagen als alle andern Gleichungen der Physik. Man ziehe etwa die Maxwell'schen Gleichungen des leeren Raumes zum Vergleich heran. Diese sind Formulierungen, die den Erfahrungen an unendlich schwachen elektromagnetischen Feldern entsprechen. Dieser empirische Ursprung bedingt schon ihre lineare Form; dass aber die wahren Gesetze nicht linear sein können, wurde schon

It is my opinion that the contemporary quantum theory represents an optimal formulation of the relationships, given certain fixed basic concepts, which by and large have been taken from classical mechanics. I believe, however, that this theory offers no useful point of departure for future development. This is the point at which my expectation deviates most widely from that of contemporary physicists. They are convinced that it is impossible to account for the essential aspects of quantum phenomena (apparently discontinuous and temporally not determined changes of the state of a system, simultaneously corpuscular and undulatory qualities of the elementary carriers of energy) by means of a theory that describes the real state of things [objects] by continuous functions of space for which differential equations are valid. They are also of the opinion that in this way one cannot understand the atomic structure of matter and of radiation. They rather expect that systems of differential equations, which might be considered for such a theory, in any case would have no solutions that would be regular (free from singularities) everywhere in four-dimensional space. Above everything else, however, they believe that the apparently discontinuous character of elementary processes can be described only by means of an essentially statistical theory, in which the discontinuous changes of the systems are accounted for by continuous changes of the probabilities of the possible states.

All of these remarks seem to me to be quite impressive. But the crux of the matter appears to me to be this question: What can be attempted with some hope of success in view of the present situation of physical theory? Here it is the experiences with the theory of gravitation that determine my expectations. In my opinion, these equations are more likely to tell us something *precise* than all other equations of physics. Take, for instance, Maxwell's equations of empty space by way of comparison. These are formulations corresponding to our experiences with infinitely weak electromagnetic fields. This empirical origin already determines their linear form; it has, however, already been emphasized above that the true laws cannot be linear. Such linear laws fulfill the superposition principle

früher betont. Solche Gesetze erfüllen das Superpositions-Prinzip für ihre Lösungen, enthalten also keine Aussagen über die Wechselwirkungen von Elementargebilden. Die wahren Gesetze können nicht linear sein und aus solchen auch nicht gewonnen werden. Noch etwas anderes habe ich aus der Gravitationstheorie gelernt: Eine noch so umfangreiche Sammlung empirischer Fakten kann nicht zur Aufstellung so verwickelter Gleichungen führen. Eine Theorie kann an der Erfahrung geprüft werden, aber es gibt keinen Weg von der Erfahrung zur Aufstellung einer Theorie. Gleichungen von solcher Kompliziertheit wie die Gleichungen des Gravitationsfeldes können nur dadurch gefunden werden, dass eine logisch einfache mathematische Bedingung gefunden wird, welche die Gleichungen völlig oder nahezu determiniert. Hat man aber jene hinreichend starken formalen Bedingungen, so braucht man nur wenig Tatsachen-Wissen für die Aufstellung der Theorie; bei den Gravitationsgleichungen ist es die Vierdimensionalität und der symmetrische Tensor als Ausdruck für die Raumstruktur, welche zusammen mit der Invarianz bezüglich der kontinuierlichen Transformationsgruppe die Gleichungen praktisch vollkommen determinieren.

Unsere Aufgabe ist es, die Feldgleichungen für das totale Feld zu finden. Die gesuchte Struktur muss eine Verallgemeinerung des symmetrischen Tensors sein. Die Gruppe darf nicht enger sein als die der kontinuierlichen Koordinaten-Transformationen. Wenn man nun eine reichere Struktur einführt, so wird die Gruppe die Gleichungen nicht mehr so stark determinieren wie im Falle des symmetrischen Tensors als Struktur. Deshalb wäre es am schönsten, wenn es gelänge, die Gruppe abermals zu erweitern in Analogie zu dem Schritte, der von der speziellen Relativität zur allgemeinen Relativität geführt hat. Im Besonderen habe ich versucht, die Gruppe der komplexen Koordinaten-Transformationen heranzuziehen. Alle derartigen Bemühungen waren erfolglos. Eine offene oder verdeckte Erhöhung der Dimensionzahl des Raumes habe ich ebenfalls aufgegeben, eine Bemühung, die von Kaluza begründet wurde und in ihrer projektiven Variante noch heute ihre Anhänger hat. Wir beschränken uns auf den vierdimensionalen Raum und die Gruppe der kontinuierlichen reellen Koordinaten-Transformationen. Nach vielen Jahren vergeblichen Suchens halte ich die im Folgenden

for their solutions; hence they contain no assertions concerning the interaction of elementary bodies. The true laws cannot be linear, nor can they be derived from such. I have learned something else from the theory of gravitation: no collection of empirical facts however comprehensive can ever lead to the setting up of such complicated equations. A theory can be tested by experience, but there is no way from experience to the construction of a theory. Equations of such complexity as are the equations of the gravitational field can be found only through the discovery of a logically simple mathematical condition that determines the equations completely or almost completely. Once one has obtained those sufficiently strong formal conditions, one requires only little knowledge of facts for the construction of the theory; in the case of the equations of gravitation it is the four-dimensionality and the symmetric tensor as expression for the structure of space that, together with the invariance with respect to the continuous transformation group, determine the equations all but completely.

Our task is that of finding the field equations for the total field. The desired structure must be a generalization of the symmetric tensor. The group must not be any narrower than that of the continuous transformations of coordinates. If one introduces a richer structure, then the group will no longer determine the equations as strongly as in the case of the symmetrical tensor as structure. Therefore it would be most beautiful if one were to succeed in expanding the group once more in analogy to the step that led from special relativity to general relativity. More specifically, I have attempted to draw upon the group of the complex transformations of the coordinates. All such endeavors were unsuccessful. I also gave up an open or concealed increase in the number of dimensions of space, an endeavor originally undertaken by Kaluza that, with its projective variant, even today has its adherents. We shall limit ourselves to the four-dimensional space and to the group of the continuous real transformations of coordinates. After many years

skizzierte Lösung für die logischerweise am meisten befriendigende.

Anstelle des symmetrischen g_{ik} ($g_{ik}=g_{ki}$) wird der nicht-symmetrische Tensor g_{ik} eingeführt. Diese Grösse setzt sich aus einem symmetrischen Teil s_{ik} und einem reellen oder gänzlich imaginären antisymmetrischen a_{ik} so zusammen:

$$g_{ik} = s_{ik} + a_{ik}.$$

Vom Standpunkte der Gruppe aus betrachtet ist diese Zusammenfügung von s and a willkürlich, weil die Tensoren s und a einzeln Tensor-Charakter haben. Es zeigt sich aber, dass diese g_{ik} (als Ganzes betrachtet) im Aufbau der neuen Theorie eine analoge Rolle spielen wie die symmetrischen g_{ik} in der Theorie des reinen Gravitationsfeldes.

Diese Verallgemeinerung der Raum-Struktur scheint auch vom Standpunkt unseres physikalischen Wissens natürlich, weil wir wissen, dass das elektromagnetische Feld mit einem schief symmetrischen Tensor zu tun hat.

Es ist ferner für die Gravitationstheorie wesentlich, dass aus den symmetrischen g_{ik} die skalare Dichte $\sqrt{|g_{ik}|}$ gebildet werden kann sowie der kontravariante Tensor g^{ik} gemäss der Definition

$$g_{ik}g^{il} = \delta_k{}^l \quad (\delta_k{}^l = \text{Kronecker-Tensor}).$$

Diese Bildungen lassen sich genau entsprechend für die nicht-symmetrischen g_{ik} definieren, ebenso Tensor-Dichten.

In der Gravitationstheorie ist es ferner wesentlich, dass sich zu einem gegebenen symmetrischen g_{ik}-Feld ein $\Gamma_{ik}{}^l$ definieren lässt, das in den unteren Indices symmetrisch ist und geometrisch betrachtet die Parallel-Verschiebung eines Vektors beherrscht. Analog lässt sich zu den nicht-symmetrischen g_{ik} ein nicht-symmetrisches $\Gamma_{ik}{}^l$ definieren, gemäss der Formel

$$g_{ik,l} - g_{sk}\Gamma_{il}{}^s - g_{is}\Gamma_{lk}{}^s = 0, \qquad \text{(A)}$$

welche mit der betreffenden Beziehung der symmetrischen g übereinstimmt, nur dass hier natürlich auf die Stellung der unteren Indices in den g und Γ geachtet werden muss.

of fruitless searching, I consider the solution sketched in what follows the one that is logically most satisfying.

In place of the symmetric g_{ik} ($g_{ik}=g_{ki}$), the nonsymmetric tensor g_{ik} is introduced. This quantity is composed of a symmetric part s_{ik} and of a real or purely imaginary antisymmetric a_{ik}, thus:

$$g_{ik}=s_{ik}+a_{ik}.$$

Viewed from the standpoint of the group, the combination of s and a is arbitrary, because the tensors s and a individually have tensor character. It turns out, however, that these g_{ik} (viewed as a whole) play a quite analogous role in the construction of the new theory to the symmetric g_{ik} in the theory of the pure gravitational field.

This generalization of the space structure seems natural also from the standpoint of our physical knowledge, because we know that the electromagnetic field involves an antisymmetric tensor.

For the theory of gravitation it is furthermore essential that from the symmetric g_{ik} it is possible to form the scalar density $\sqrt{|g_{ik}|}$ as well as the contravariant tensor g_{ik} according to the definition

$$g_{ik}g^{il}=\delta_k{}^l \quad (\delta_k{}^l=\text{Kronecker tensor}).$$

These structures can be defined in precise correspondence for the nonsymmetric g_{ik}, including tensor densities.

In the theory of gravitation it is further essential that, for a given symmetric g_{ik}-field, a field $\Gamma_{ik}{}^l$ can be defined, which is symmetric in the subscripts and which, considered geometrically, governs the parallel displacement of a vector. Analogously for the nonsymmetric g_{ik} a nonsymmetric $\Gamma_{ik}{}^l$ can be defined, according to the formula

$$g_{ik,l}-g_{sk}\Gamma_{il}{}^s-g_{is}\Gamma_{lk}{}^s=0, \tag{A}$$

which accords with the corresponding relation of the symmetric g, only that, of course, one must pay attention here to the position of the lower indices in the g and Γ.

Wie in der reellen Theorie kann aus den Γ eine Krümmung $R_{klm}{}^i$ gebildet werden und aus dieser eine kontrahierte Krümmung R_{kl}. Endlich kann man unter Verwendung eine Variationsprinzips mit (A) zusammen kompatible Feldgleichungen finden:

$$\mathfrak{g}^{is}{}_{,s} = 0 \quad (\mathfrak{g}^{ik} = \tfrac{1}{2}(g^{ik} - g^{ki})\ \sqrt{-|g_{ik}|}\ ) \tag{B_1}$$

$$\Gamma_{i\underset{\smile}{s}}{}^s = 0 \quad (\Gamma_{i\underset{\smile}{s}}{}^s = \tfrac{1}{2}(\Gamma_{is}{}^s - \Gamma_{si}{}^s)) \tag{B_2}$$

$$R_{\underline{ik}} = 0 \tag{C_1}$$

$$R_{k\underset{\smile}{l},m} + R_{l\underset{\smile}{m},k} + R_{m\underset{\smile}{k},l} = 0 \tag{C_2}$$

Hierbei ist jede der beiden Gleichungen (B₁), (B₂) eine Folge der andern, wenn (A) erfüllt ist. $R_{\underline{kl}}$ bedeutet den symmetrischen, $R_{k\underset{\smile}{l}}$ den antisymmetrischen Teil von R_{kl}.

Im Falle des Verschwindens des antisymmetrischen Teils von g_{ik} reduzieren sich diese Formeln auf (A) und (C₁) –Fall des reinen Gravitationsfeldes.

Ich glaube, dass diese Gleichungen die natürlichste Verallgemeinerung der Gravitationsgleichungen darstellen.[2] Die Prüfung ihrer physikalischen Brauchbarkeit ist eine überaus schwierige Aufgabe, weil es mit Annäherungen nicht getan ist. Die Frage ist: Was für im ganzen Raume singularitätsfreie Lösungen dieser Gleichungen gibt es?

Diese Darlegung hat ihren Zweck erfüllt, wenn sie dem Leser zeigen, wie die Bemühungen eines Lebens miteinander zusammenhängen und warum sie zu Erwartungen bestimmter Art geführt haben.

A. Einstein.

Institute for Advanced Study
Princeton, New Jersey

---

[2] Die hier vorgeschlagene Theorie hat nach meiner Ansicht ziemliche Wahrscheinlichkeit der Bewährung, wenn sich der Weg einer erschöpfenden Darstellung der physischen Realität auf der Grundlage des Kontinuums überhaupt als gangbar erweisen wird.

Just as in the theory with symmetric g_{ik}, it is possible to form a curvature $R_{klm}{}^i$ out of the Γ, and from it a contracted curvature R_{kl}. Finally, by employing a variational principle together with (A), it is possible to find compatible field equations:

$$\mathfrak{g}^{\underline{i s}}{}_{,s} = 0 \quad (\mathfrak{g}^{\underline{i k}} = \tfrac{1}{2}\,(g^{ik} - g^{ki})\,\sqrt{-|g_{ik}|}\,) \tag{B$_1$}$$

$$\Gamma_{\underline{i s}}{}^s = 0 \quad (\Gamma_{\underline{i s}}{}^s = \tfrac{1}{2}\,(\Gamma_{is}{}^s - \Gamma_{si}{}^s)) \tag{B$_2$}$$

$$R_{\underline{i k}} = 0 \tag{C$_1$}$$

$$R_{\underline{k l},m} + R_{\underline{l m},k} + R_{\underline{m k},l} = 0 \tag{C$_2$}$$

Each of the two equations (B$_1$), (B$_2$) is a consequence of the other if (A) is satisfied. $R_{\underline{k l}}$ denotes the symmetric, $R_{\underline{k l}}$ the antisymmetric part of R_{kl}.

If the antisymmetric part of g_{ik} vanishes, these formulas reduce to (A) and (C$_1$) – the case of the pure gravitational field.

I believe that these equations constitute the most natural generalization of the equations of gravitation.[2] The proof of their physical usefulness is a tremendously difficult task, inasmuch as mere approximations will not suffice. The question is: What solutions do these equations have that are regular everywhere?

This exposition has fulfilled its purpose if it shows the reader how the efforts of a life hang together and why they have led to expectations of a certain kind.

A. Einstein.

Institute for Advanced Study
Princeton, New Jersey
[ca. 1946]

---

[2] The theory here proposed, according to my view, has a fair probability of being found valid, if the way to an exhaustive description of physical reality on the basis of the continuum turns out to be at all feasible.

Printed in the USA
CPSIA information can be obtained
at www.ICGtesting.com
JSHW012017140824
68134JS00025B/2464

9 780812 691795